Making Trouble

Making Trouble:
Surrealism and the Human Sciences

Derek Sayer

PRICKLY PARADIGM PRESS
CHICAGO

In memory of Daniel Nugent (1954-1997)

Prickly Paradigm Press, LLC
5629 South University Avenue
Chicago, IL 60637

www.prickly-paradigm.com

ISBN: 9780996635523
LCCN: 2017934555

Printed in the United States of America on acid-free paper.

Around 1905 Picasso acquires a West African mask. It is beautiful, all planes and cylinders. He discovers cubism.

—James Clifford, *The Predicament of Culture*

Contents

Preface

This essay started life as the 2015 Annual Methods Lab Lecture at Goldsmiths College, University of London. It was an invitation I was more than happy to accept, not least because the Methods Lab described itself as "a laboratory for the practice of sociological imagination." My original plan had been to use the lecture as an opportunity to clarify—for myself, perhaps, as much as others—why I had given my book *Prague: Capital of the Twentieth Century* (2013) the subtitle *A Surrealist History*. Beyond a brief preliminary discussion of Walter Benjamin's *Arcades Project*, whose attempt to grasp the modern condition through a montage of images rather than a chronological narrative or a coherent argument had informed both my title and my approach, I had said very little in the book itself about questions of theory or method. *Making Trouble* has since become much more than a gloss on *Prague, Capital of the Twentieth Century*. As one thing led to another the text evolved into a freewheeling exploration of what surrealism as an "instrument of knowledge" (as Paul Éluard called it) might offer the human sciences—in which I include sociology and history, the academic disciplines in which I have spent my career, as well as anthropology, whose connections with surrealism have been long recognized by James Clifford, Michael Taussig, and others. It is probably the nearest thing to an intellectual credo I am ever to write.

Like much of my work over the last two decades this book has one foot in academia and the other in the arts. It is a creative tension I have found extraordinarily productive, which informed both *Prague* and its predecessor *The Coasts of Bohemia: A Czech History* (1998). But I am also well aware that as far as governments, funding agencies, and university managers are concerned I am swimming against the current. The methodological vagrancy I am advocating here is not likely to help anyone win research grants, publish in top-ranked journals, or get 4-star rankings for their "outputs" in the United Kingdom's fatuously misnamed Research Excellence Framework (REF). I have written this essay at the point of my formal retirement from a university system for whose future I am deeply pessimistic, not just because of the philistine depredations of politicians on both sides of the Atlantic but because of senior academics' willingness to strike Faustian bargains with agendas driven by income-generation and impact. When Susan Sontag was asked in 1995 by *Paris Review* whether she thought that "being an academic and being a creative writer are incompatible," she replied: "Yes. Worse than incompatible. I've seen academic life destroy the best writers of my generation." Once upon a time I would have strongly disagreed with her. Nowadays I fear she was right. Spaces for academics to be creative are fast disappearing—to our collective cultural loss.

I would like to thank Mariam Motamedi-Fraser and Nirmal Puwar for organizing the event at Goldsmiths, as well as the audience for a stimulating hour-long discussion after the lecture. Craig Campbell, Karen Engle, Ben Highmore, Mark Jackson, John Jervis, Béatrice Joyeux-Prunel, Randolph Lewis, Vanessa Longden, Kimberly Mair, Michael Richardson, Benjamin Tallis, Jindřich Toman, and Yoke-Sum Wong all offered comments or advice on this text. I am deeply grateful for their support. After several rejections from publishers who found my manuscript too long for an article, too short for a book, or too idiosyncratic for present-day academic tastes, I owe particular thanks to Matthew Engelke and Marshall Sahlins at Prickly Paradigm for taking on this project. I am honored to be part of what has over the years become a pioneering venue for heretical voices in the academy. I hope my book matches the standards of prickliness set by the series, as well as contributing to the case for bringing imagination back to the human sciences.

Calgary, Alberta
5 July 2016

Prologue—
New York, December 1936

"Surrealism may amuse you, it may shock you, it may scandalize you, but one thing is certain: you will not be able to ignore it," promised a Faber and Faber advertisement for André Breton's *What Is Surrealism*, a pamphlet it (wrongly) claimed the surrealist leader had "written especially for the first International Surrealist Exhibition to be held in London." Readers were assured that Breton's text revealed surrealism "not as one more little sectarian affair designed to flutter the cafes of London and Paris, but as a deliberate and even a desperate attempt to transform the world." The exhibition, which ran from 11 June to 4 July 1936 at the New Burlington Galleries in Mayfair, has been better remembered since for Sheila Legge wandering Trafalgar Square in a torn white dress and facemask covered in roses as "the phantom of sex appeal" and Salvador Dalí nearly suffocating while giving a lecture in a deep-sea diving suit intended to represent a descent into his unconscious. But Herbert Read was nevertheless probably right that "when the foam and froth of society and the press had subsided, we were left with a serious public of scientists, artists, philosophers and socialists." Beneath the stunts and the showboating surrealism was a deeply serious intellectual movement.

The foam and froth had meantime crossed the Atlantic. "One sure thing, you aren't going to find a solitary place to hide from surrealism this winter," warned *Harper's Bazaar*. *Fantastic Art, Dada, Surrealism*, which opened on 7 December 1936 at the Museum of Modern Art, "turned out to be the most discussed exhibition in New York since the Armory Show of 1913." Coney Island came to Manhattan in all its vulgarity and enchantment. *Fantastic Art* played havoc with the boundaries between high art and popular culture, indecently muddling the avant-garde and kitsch. "Inside the front door of Manhattan's Museum of Modern Art this week," began *Time*'s December 14 cover story,

> oblong slabs of glass painted with black stripes revolved steadily under a six foot pair of red lips painted by Artist Man Ray. In other galleries throughout the building were a black felt head with a necklace of cinema film and zippers for eyes; a stuffed parrot on a hollow log containing a doll's leg; a teacup, plate and spoon covered entirely with fur.

The cover featured a Man Ray photograph of Salvador Dalí with the caption: "SURREALIST SALVADOR DALÍ—A blazing pine, an archbishop, a giraffe, and a cloud of feathers went out the window."

Julien Levy, whose Madison Avenue gallery had first introduced New York to surrealism four years earlier, cashed in on the brouhaha with an "art book, anthology, lexicon, and manifesto" (with a cover by Queens homeboy Joseph Cornell) titled *Surrealism* and an exhibition of Dalí's latest paintings. It was the Catalan artist's fourth solo show at the gallery in as many years. Dalí was the perfect poster boy for surrealism as show business. His apotheosis would come three years later at the 1939 New York World's Fair, where he refused to exhibit in the official beaux-arts spaces and instead parked his "Dreams of Venus" pavilion in the Amusement Zone alongside the Wall of Death, the Drop of Doom, and a "Cuban Village" that promised "a completely nude girl in its voodoo sacrifice routine at the first show of opening day." In hindsight, Dalí's perverse cocktail of melting watches, burning giraffes, and topless "living liquid ladies" seems better attuned to the darkening times than the Fair's facile slogan "Building the World of Tomorrow with the Tools of Today" and futuristic illusions of the Perisphere and Trylon. World War II was six months away.

    Fantastic Art, Dada, Surrealism was a bold venture for MoMA and its curator Alfred Barr, breaking with the rationalism of the modernist canon that the museum had sought to define through its earlier exhibitions *The International Style* (1932), *The Machine Age* (1934), and *Cubism and Abstract Art* (1936). Barr admitted that "*Cubism and Abstract Art* was ... diametrically opposed in both spirit and esthetic principles" to *Fantastic Art.* His cover for *Cubism and Abstract Art* charts the evolution of modern art from Japanese prints, Van Gogh, neo-impressionism, and Cézanne through cubism, futurism, and expressionism to geometric and non-geometric abstraction. *Fantastic Art* surveyed a more chaotic landscape—but one that in retrospect also offered a more prescient intimation of what the rest of the century and its arts had in store than the "skeletal clarity and purity of [Barr's] diagram." The focus of *Fantastic Art* was not on what is new in modernity but "the deep-seated and persistent interest which human beings have in the fantastic, the irrational, the spontaneous, the marvelous, the enigmatic, and the dreamlike."

Where *Cubism and Abstract Art* had carried the torch for "a Brave New World of art ... belonging to our century and to no other," *Fantastic Art* located surrealism within an atavistic trajectory that led back through Blake and Goya to Arcimboldo and Hieronymus Bosch—though Barr optimistically suggested that "many of the fantastic and apparently Surrealist works of the Baroque or Renaissance are to be explained on *rational* grounds rather than on a *Surrealist* basis of subconscious and irrational expression." He also included the "art of children" and the "art of the insane" in the exhibition, noting "many children and psychopaths exist ... in a world of their own unattainable to the rest of us save in art or dreams in which the imagination lives an unfettered life." This unwittingly foreshadowed the Nazis' venomous display of drawings by children and psychiatric patients in the infamous *Degenerate "Art"* exhibition of 1938, whose intention was to show that the "specific *intellectual ideal*" of modern art was "the *idiot*, the *cretin*, and the *cripple*" ("the *Negro* and the *South Sea Islander*," the catalogue added, was its "evident *racial ideal*"). We are entering a terrain where the boundaries between an enlightened modernity and the dark ages that preceded it are uncertain. *Fantastic Art, Dada, Surrealism* could as well have been titled the return of the repressed, and maybe it should have been given what was happening at the time in Europe. It was, after all, the year of the Berlin Olympics.

Despite his own modernist predilections, Barr acknowledged "It is probable that at no time in the past four hundred years has the art of the marvelous and anti-rational been more conspicuous than at the present time." This begs the obvious question—though Barr never asked it—of what it was about the period between the two World Wars that made surrealist art so popular when on the face of it we might have expected the classical modernist perspectives championed by MoMA to be better suited to the cultural expression of the *Zeitgeist*. But surrealism always dug beneath the face of things. Barr is right to stress that surrealism is as modern a movement as cubism, futurism, or the International Style rather than merely a continuation of a universal human fascination with the fantastic. But unlike other early twentieth-century -isms, it articulates the dark side of the force, seeking to bring to consciousness what modernist grand narratives of history-as-progress—including narratives of the Cartesian rational subject, a fantasy already undermined (as the surrealists well understood) by Sigmund Freud—had suppressed. World War I let slip the demons of modernity. Dada and surrealism were responses to the resulting crisis of western culture— modernity's dissident self-consciousness, we might say. After the brief interlude of the jazz age the Great Crash of 1929 headed things downhill again until by 1936 dreamscapes of the fantastic loomed ever larger over the horizons of the real. The Holocaust and Hiroshima were waiting in the wings.

The surrealists always insisted that surrealism was an instrument of knowledge rather than just a literary or artistic movement. A central part of their critique of the white, western, bourgeois civilization they had come to despise was a sustained challenge to modern scientific rationality as a privileged vehicle for understanding the world. In this respect they anticipated some of the core arguments of later postcolonial and feminist perspectives, seeking to provincialize the privileged standpoints from which knowledge is usually derived. *Making Trouble* explores what taking this claim seriously might entail for the human sciences. Like an earlier explorer of this terrain, Ben Highmore, I treat surrealism as "a form of social research into everyday life" and "see its products not as works of art but as documents of this social research. In this way artistic techniques such as collage become methodologies for attending to the social." In the course of this discussion I draw upon a broad array of sociological, anthropological, and cultural theorists as well as creative writers, artists, and photographers. Among them are Roland Barthes, Robert K. Merton, Paul Feyerabend, Harold Garfinkel, Emile Durkheim, Milan Kundera, Susan Sontag, Georges Bataille, James Clifford, Michel Leiris, Claude Lévi-Strauss, Aimé Césaire, Humphrey Jennings, Tom Harrisson, Walter Benjamin, Eduardo Galleano, and Horace Walpole—plus a large contingent of Dada and surrealist writers and artists. Above all there is the towering figure of André Breton. It is my hope that (to borrow a concept from Milan Kundera) we may find density in their unexpected encounters.

All were in their different ways troublemakers; all would have subscribed to Gaston Bachelard's dictum "*In the domain of thought imprudence is a method.*" None would have been seen dead following the painting-by-numbers recipe for knowledge production, taken from the website of Britain's national research funding agency for the social sciences, with which this essay begins—a nadir of the contemporary academic imagination that suggests Max Weber was right a century ago to end *The Protestant Ethic* with his fears of a future of "mechanized petrification, embellished with a sort of convulsive self-importance," in which "specialists without spirit, sensualists without heart" rule the roost. Bachelard held the inaugural chair in history and philosophy of sciences at the Sorbonne. It is entirely to the point, however, that I quote him here not from an academic journal but from an article published in *Inquisitions*, an avant-garde magazine edited by onetime surrealists Louis Aragon, Roger Caillois, and Tristan Tzara. The article first appeared in English—alongside Samuel Beckett's translations of Paul Éluard's poems, film scenarios for Luis Buñuel and Salvador Dalí's *The Andalusian Dog* and Joseph Cornell's *Monsieur Phot*, and illustrations from Max Ernst's collage-novel *A Little Girl Dreams of Taking the Veil*—in Julien Levy's anthology *Surrealism*, published to illuminate what was going on the year Coney Island came to Manhattan.

Making Trouble

1
An Accidental Sagacity

The United Kingdom's national funding agency for research in the social sciences, the Economic and Social Research Council (ESRC), begins its guidelines for grant writing with the seemingly obvious advice: "Make sure you think your plan through and cover all stages." Among the questions applicants are recommended to ask themselves are the following—

- Have I clearly formulated the problem ... put it in context of contemporary scientific and theoretical debates, demonstrated the way in which my work will build on existing research and make a contribution to the area? Is there a clear and convincingly argued analytical framework?
- Have I provided a well thought out research design in which there is a reasoned explanation of the scale, timing and resources necessary?
- Have I given a full and detailed description of the proposed research methods?

- Have I demonstrated a clear and systematic approach to the analysis of data?

What is curious about this checklist (which is typical of the genre) is just how much ESRC expects to have been "thought through" before the research has been undertaken. That any or all of these things might be changed, perhaps fundamentally, by the process of research itself in ways that could not have been foreseen at the start seems never to have been considered. But in the words of the impeccably dead, white, and male doyen of American sociology Robert K. Merton, "Fruitful empirical research not only tests theoretically-derived hypotheses; it also originates new hypotheses. This might be called the 'serendipity' component in research, i.e., *the discovery, by chance or sagacity, of valid results which were not sought for.*" I would add that the process of research might give rise to equally unanticipated sources of data, methods of inquiry, and frameworks of analysis too. It might indeed be suggested that research that is not capable of generating such discoveries is not worth funding—and that any research design worth its salt should build in openness to serendipity.

It is rare that we are able to give a precise origin to words, but it was Horace Walpole, youngest son of Great Britain's first Prime Minister Robert Walpole, who coined the term "serendipity" in a letter to his friend Horace Mann of 28 January 1754. Walpole is best remembered today for the intimate portrait of eighteenth-century upper-class English life painted in his voluminous letters, the "Gothic castle" he built at Strawberry Hill in the Thames valley west of London to house his remarkable collection of "furniture, pictures, curiosities, &c.," and his authorship of the first Gothic novel *The Castle of Otranto*. ESRC would not have been impressed by *Otranto*'s method of composition. Walpole awoke one morning, he says, from a dream of which "all I could recover was, that I had thought myself in an ancient castle ... and that on the uppermost banister of a great staircase I saw a gigantic hand in armour. In the evening I sat down and began to write, *without knowing in the least what I intended to say or relate*." The dream was likely inspired by the hall and staircase at Strawberry Hill, which Walpole reckoned "the most particular and chief beauty of the castle."

The provenance of the concept of serendipity turns out to be every bit as whimsical as the caprice of circumstance to which it gives a name. "You will understand it better," Walpole tells Mann, "by the derivation than by the definition":

> I once read a silly fairy tale, called *the three princes of Serendip*: as their Highnesses travelled, they were always making discoveries, by accidents and sagacity, of things which they were not in quest of: for instance, one of them discovered that a mule blind of the right eye had travelled the same road lately, because the grass was eaten only on the left side, where it was worse than on the right—now do you understand *Serendipity*?

Walpole emphasizes that serendipity is an "accidental sagacity," for "*no* discovery of a thing you are looking for comes under this description." As Edward Solly clarified in *Notes and Queries* over a century later, "'Serendipity,' as the word was used by Walpole, meant the discovery of things which the finder was not in search of."

There are two sides to serendipity thus understood. On the side of the subject, there is Walpole's "sagacity." Those hoping for the blessings of serendipity need to cultivate a "receptive eye." It is the unexpected, the incongruous, the anomalous, in a word *the Odd*—in this case, the fact that the grass by the roadside was cropped only on the left, where it was inferior—that draws their attention. To adapt a well-known distinction Roland Barthes makes apropos photography, this is the *punctum* that pricks the *studium*, upsetting our preconceptions and expectations. In this context, thinking plans through in advance and covering all stages is unlikely to be helpful. Indeed, it may well be counterproductive. Serendipity requires "Curiosity, wonder, *openness*— [and] these cohabit, comfortably, in that marvelous coinage of Walpole." But not every photograph has a *punctum* and anomalies cannot be conjured up to order. So the other side of serendipity is what Walpole calls "accident" and André Breton dubbed "objective chance" (*hasard objectif*), a key concept in the surrealist lexicon. *Hasard objectif*, Breton told the audience in a lecture on "The Surrealist Situation of the Object" in Prague in 1935, is "that sort of chance that shows man, in a way that is still very mysterious, a necessity that escapes him, even though he experiences it as a vital necessity." Think of Archimedes and the bath, Newton and the apple, Alexander Fleming and a Petri dish contaminated with mold.

I am drawing here on Robert K. Merton and Elinor Barber's book *The Travels and Adventures of Serendipity*. Merton and Barber's wanderings through the history of serendipity admirably exemplify its authors' sense of the contingency of all things, transporting us from Christoforo Armeno's *Peregrinaggio di tre giovani figlivoli del Re di Serendippo*—the source for Walpole's "silly fairy tale"—in Venice in 1557, through the names of cruise lines and London book-stores, advertisements for pharmaceutical companies and the corridors of the Harvard Medical School, to an Australian ranch and a nudist camp outside Atlanta, Georgia. Completed in 1958, the manuscript was "set aside ... for a while" while Merton turned his attention to writing the no less peripatetic *On the Shoulders of Giants*, which is a history (of sorts) of Isaac Newton's aphorism "If I have seen further, it is by standing on the shoulders of giants." By the time *Travels and Adventures* found its way into print—in Italian—in 2002, Elinor Barber was dead and Merton, against all rational expectations, had celebrated his ninety-first birthday. He died the following year. Princeton University Press finally published *The Travels and Adventures of Serendipity* in English in 2004.

In his 1985 Preface to *On the Shoulders of Giants* Robert Merton identifies what he calls "the determining ancestor of this prodigal brainchild of mine." It is not, perhaps, what we might ordinarily expect from a founding father of structural-functional-ist sociology:

> As I now reconstruct [the book's] origins, I adopted the non-linear, advancing-by-doubling-back Shandean Method of composition at the same time I was reflecting that *this open form resembles the course taken by history in general*, by the history of ideas in particular, and, in a way, by the course taken in scientific inquiry as well. For a lifelong addict of [Laurence Sterne's] *The Life and Opinions of Tristram Shandy, Gentleman*, this complex hypothesis inexorably brought to mind the graphic depiction, in Book VI, Chapter XL, of the eccentric trajectory followed by the first four of its pathmak-ing volumes along these exact lines:

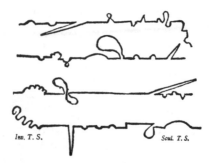

Inv. T. S.   *Scul. T. S.*

Like Walpole in *The Castle of Otranto*, Sterne began his itinerary with no very clear idea of where his journey would take him. What Merton calls the "canonical passage in the Shandean scripture" is this:

> That of all the several ways of beginning a book that are now in practice throughout the known world, I am confident that my own way of doing it is the best—I'm sure it is the most religious,—for I begin with writing the first sentence,—and trusting to Almighty God for the second.

Merton insists that the importance of the "Shandean Method that is not a method" is by no means confined to the creative arts. "As I strongly affirmed almost twenty years ago—doubtless benefiting from a miscellany of Shandean insights—work in the sciences also commonly proceeds in anything but inexorably linear style." There is, he says, a "rock-bound difference between the finished versions of scientific work as they appear in print and the actual course of inquiry followed by the inquirer":

> The difference is a little like that between textbooks on "scientific method" and the ways in which scientists actually think, feel, and go about their work.

The books on methods present ideal patterns: how scientists ought to think, feel and act, but these tidy normative patterns, as everyone who has engaged in [such] inquiry knows, do not reproduce the typically untidy, opportunistic adaptations that scientists make in the course of their inquiries. Typically, the scientific paper or monograph presents an immaculate appearance which reproduces nothing of the intuitive leaps, false starts, mistakes, loose ends and happy accidents that actually cluttered up the inquiry.

Paul Feyerabend advanced a similar argument in *Against Method*, which he provocatively subtitled *Outline of an Anarchistic Theory of Knowledge*. Challenged on his blasphemous observation "anything goes," Feyerabend responded:

"Anything goes" is not a "principle" I hold—I do not think that "principles" can be used and fruitfully discussed outside the concrete research situation they are supposed to affect—but *the terrified exclamation of a rationalist who takes a closer look at history.*

Be warned.

2
The Bureau of Surrealist Research

Against the sterile protocols exemplified by ESRC's recipe for successful grant-writing (as distinct from fruitful research), I wish to advocate the importance of what Teju Cole has called "vagrancy, the freedom to drift, the right to look at things from outside the mainstream." What, then, might a sociology (or an anthropology, or a history) driven by "curiosity, wonder, openness"—a sociology that is open to the whimsies of serendipity and the hazards of objective chance and willing to follow the divagating course of the Shandean method—look like? The Bureau for Surrealist Research, which opened at 15, rue de Grenelle in Paris on 11 October 1924, four days before André Breton published the first *Manifesto of Surrealism*, furnishes one possible methodological antecedent. Though surrealism is commonly regarded as a literary or artistic movement, the surrealists always insisted that (in the words of Paul Éluard, lecturing on "Poetic Evidence" at the International Surrealist Exhibition in London in 1936) surrealism is "an *instrument of knowledge* ... that strives to bring to light man's profound consciousness." The Bureau was intended to provide "an open door on *the unknown*, this *unknown* in which the surrealists place all their hope."

The surrealists' objective, stated the press release for the opening, was to gather "all the information possible relating to forms that might express the unconscious activity of the mind." The announcement reads like a pastiche of a call for academic papers. "No domain has been specified, a priori, for this undertaking," it explains, "and surrealism proposes a gathering of the greatest possible number of experimental elements *for a purpose that cannot yet be perceived*":

> All those who have the means to contribute, in any fashion, to the creation of genuine surrealist archives, are *urgently requested* to come forward: let them shed light on the genesis of an invention, or propose a new system of psychic investigation, or make us the judges of striking coincidences, or reveal their most instinctive ideas on fashion, as well as politics, etc., or freely criticize morality, or even simply entrust us with their most curious dreams ...

Two people staffed the ground-floor office of the "Centrale" from 4:30 to 6:30 on a daily rota (except for Sundays), keeping a *Cahier de la permanence* recording the day's activities and the names and addresses of visitors. Upstairs was a room where members of the group could meet, discuss, or work on their individual projects. Simone Breton made an initial inventory on October 12 recording the presence of paintings by De Chirico, Max Morise, and Robert Desnos, books by André Breton, Louis Aragon,

Benjamin Péret, and Pierre Naville, the proofs of the *Manifesto of Surrealism*, a Bible, and a typewriter. Two days later André Breton noted down the arrival of vitrines by Man Ray, Louis Aragon requested that somebody check out "a poster noticed by Jean Paulhan titled IT IS NECESSARY TO TAKE THE SIDE OF THE DEVIL, which can be found on the boulevard Raspail opposite the Librarie de France," and Pierre Naville asked that "people preferably throw dead matches and cigarette butts in the ashtrays." Breton and Aragon spent October 20 "decorating the Centrale: a wild boar on the staircase, sundry phantoms, the Chance bell [*la cloche Hasard*] and a thought of Berkeley's." "An atmosphere of effervescent research reigned," writes Gérard Durozoi in his *History of the Surrealist Movement*,

> where the gifts of chance were always welcome ... along with the marvelous, thought to be ever latent in everyday life and ready to suggest incongruous juxtapositions of objects and arouse the imagination by reinforcing the victory over mental habits.

Much of the activity at the Bureau revolved around the surrealists' new journal *La Révolution Surréaliste*, of which twelve numbers would be published between 1925 and 1929. The first issue came out on 1 December 1924. "Surrealism doesn't present itself as the exposition of a doctrine," readers were forewarned:

> Ideas that currently serve it as a point of departure in no way permit us to prejudge its later development. Thus, this first number of *La Révolution Surréaliste* does not offer any definitive revelation ... It is necessary to wait for what is to come.

As Breton had explained a couple of months earlier, "a poem by Reverdy is systematic, in the same way that a battle plan is systematic. *For us, there is no battle plan.*" The issue included accounts of dreams by Giorgio De Chirico and André Breton, "surrealist texts" by Robert Desnos, Benjamin Péret, Paul Éluard, S. B. (Simone Breton?), Louis Aragon and others, and illustrations by Picasso, Max Ernst, and André Masson. Man Ray contributed a double exposure of a woman's breasts. But much more scandalous was a photomontage featuring Germaine Berton, the young anarchist who had shot and killed the editorial secretary of *L'Action française* the previous year, surrounded by twenty-eight "surrealists"—one of whom was Sigmund Freud, co-opted without his knowledge or permission. The montage was captioned with a quotation from Baudelaire, chosen by Paul Éluard: "Woman is the being who projects the greatest shadow or the greatest light on our dreams." Despite abundant evidence that the crime was premeditated the jury unanimously acquitted Berton at the end of her trial. The next day Louis Aragon, Simone Breton, and Max Morise took her a bouquet of red roses and carnations with a card reading "To Germaine Berton, who has done what we were unable to do."

An excellent case can be made for regarding scandal as a principal surrealist research method. The surrealists, Breton taunted in the *Second Manifesto of Surrealism*,

> intend to savor fully the profound grief, so well played, with which the bourgeois public ... greets the steadfast and unyielding need they display to laugh like savages in the presence of the French flag, to vomit their disgust in the face of every priest, and

to level at the breed of "basic duties" the long-range weapon of sexual cynicism.

In December 1926 *La Révolution Surréaliste* carried a photograph of "Our collaborator Benjamin Péret insulting a priest," followed by a reproduction of Ernst's sacrilegious painting of the Virgin Mary spanking the bare-bottomed infant Jesus. If Antonin Artaud's "Address to the Pope" exemplifies one mode of surrealist offense ("The world is the abyss of the soul, warped Pope ... Let us swim in our bodies, leave our souls within our souls, we have no need of your knife of enlightenment"), the pornographic caricature of post-office and firefighters' annual almanacs clandestinely published three years later in Brussels under the title *1929* epitomizes another. Man Ray illustrates the four seasons with close-up photographs of his intimacies with Kiki de Montparnasse, to the accompaniment of blasphemous poems by Louis Aragon and Benjamin Péret.

The surrealists showed up in force at *Mercure de France*'s celebratory banquet for the symbolist poet Saint-Pol Roux on 2 July 1925, placing an Open Letter to Paul Claudel, France's ambassador to Japan, under each plate. Claudel had recently insulted surrealism as "pederastic" while simultaneously affirming the compatibility of being a "writer, diplomat, French ambassador and poet." The letter began: "We hope with all our strength that revolution, war and colonial insurrection will annihilate this western civilization whose vermin you defend all the way to the far East." The surrealists had signed an appeal published the same day in the communist newspaper *L'Humanité* condemning France's armed intervention in the Rif Rebellion in Morocco on behalf of Spain and proclaiming "the right of peoples, of *all* peoples, of whatever race, to self-determination." "Very soon," relates Durozoi,

> voices were raised, then fistfights broke out, and soon the police were sent for ... [Michel] Leiris, who shouted "Down with France!" and "Long live Germany!" from the window, then down on the sidewalk, barely escaped a lynching.

The logic of such provocations anticipates— albeit in an extreme form—the social psychologists' breaching experiment, a research technique that deliberately flouts the implicit norms of social life in order to bring them to (often explosive) consciousness. The terms in which Harold Garfinkel classically described his method of "making commonplace scenes visible" in *Studies in Ethnomethodology* bear very close reading in this context:

> Procedurally it is my preference to start with familiar scenes and ask *what can be done to make trouble*. The operations that one would have to perform in order to multiply the senseless features of perceived environments; *to produce and sustain bewilderment, consternation, and confusion*; to produce the socially structured affects of anxiety, shame, guilt, and indignation; and to produce disorganized interaction should tell us something about how the structures of everyday activities are ordinarily and routinely produced and maintained ... my studies are not properly speaking experimental. They are demonstrations, designed, in Herbert Spiegelberg's phrase, as "aids to a sluggish imagination." I have found that they produce reflections through which *the strangeness of an obstinately familiar world can be detected*.

3
Systematic Bewildering

The "Investigation" launched in the first issue of *La Révolution Surréaliste* employed the more conventional sociological method of the questionnaire. The topic, suicide, was something of an obsession for surrealists, as it had been for Émile Durkheim in what is universally acknowledged to be a foundational text of scientific sociology. There was more to this shared interest than coincidence. Durkheim and the surrealists both rejected the commonsense presumption that suicide was an act of individual volition and therefore essentially a moral question:

INVESTIGATION
Addressing itself to all without distinction, *La Révolution Surréaliste* is inaugurating the following investigation:
One lives, one dies. What part does the will play in all this? It would seem that one kills oneself like

one dreams. This is not a moral question we are posing:

IS SUICIDE A SOLUTION?

Responses received at the Bureau of Surrealist Research, it was promised, would be published in the next issue. They duly were, prefaced by the tart observation: "There is nothing more muddled than man: if you ask him one question he answers another, or puts the question itself on trial. Do we have the right to ask if suicide is a solution? Messieurs, you get a zero." Breton's own answer—a penetrating one—was that "Suicide is a poorly made word: what kills is not identical to what is killed."

The open-ended survey became a favorite surrealist tool for researching such topics as "Why do you write?" "What do you do when you are alone?" "What kind of hope do you put in love?" and "What was the most important meeting of your life?" A 1958 "Inquiry into Striptease" asked (with separate questions for male and female respondents) whether striptease does not "in fact ... 'desexualize' woman," as Roland Barthes suggested in *Mythologies*. The most famous of these investigations was the brutally frank exploration of sexuality involving both male and female members of the Paris surrealist group that took place over at least a dozen soirées between 1928 and 1932. *La Révolution Surréaliste* published verbatim transcripts of the first two discussions alongside extracts from Breton's *Nadja* and a celebration of "the fiftieth anniversary of hysteria, the greatest poetic discovery of the end of the nineteenth century." The anniversary in question was the admission of "*La délicieuse* X. L. (Augustine)"—fifteen-year-old Louise Augustine Gleizes—to la Salpêtrière mental hospital as a patient of the renowned neurologist Jean-Martin Charcot on 21 October 1875. "Hysteria is not a pathological phenomenon and may, in all respects, be considered as a supreme means of expression," contend Breton and Aragon. They illustrated their text with photographs of a young woman in the grip of hysterical convulsions taken from Charcot's *Iconographie photographique de la Salpêtrière*.

The Bureau of Surrealist Research disbanded in April 1925. But over the next few years the surrealists pioneered a multitude of ways to uncover "the actual functioning of thought ... in the absence of any control exercised by reason, exempt from any aesthetic or moral concern," indiscriminately mixing media and disciplines and upsetting apple carts wherever they went. They took deliberately directionless strolls through nondescript areas of Paris, anticipating the Situationists' *dérive* (drift)—a technique for mapping urban psychogeographies designed to disrupt the well-trodden paths of habitus, in which

> one or more persons during a certain period drop their relations, their work and leisure activities, and all their other usual motives for movement and action, and let themselves be drawn by the attractions of the terrain and the encounters they find there.

They hung out in cheap cinemas and shabby dance halls hoping for "the descent into what in *Nadja* was referred to, positively, as the 'lower depths of the spirit.'" The same "resonant sexual overtones," Gérard Durozoi believes, "surely encouraged certain members of the group to frequent the Bal Nègre on the rue Blomet or, for some, to become regulars, like Leiris, at the cabarets where black jazz musicians played." The fruits of this ethnographic *flâneurie* can be sampled in Louis Aragon's *Paris Peasant*, Philippe Soupault's *Last Nights of Paris*, and André Breton's *Nadja*—indispensable guides to Parisian modernity in the years after World War I, charting the bygone dreamworlds of a no-man's land located somewhere between Baudelaire's "Painter of Modern Life" and Walter Benjamin's *Arcades Project*.

They drifted through flea markets hoping to stumble upon *objets trouvés* that (in Breton's words) "go off to dream at the antique fair ... nourishing the meditation that this place arouses ... concerning the precarious fate of so many little human constructions." They assassinated the author through automatic writing, trances, recordings of dreams, and games of chance. They dethroned the artist with collage, frottage, and decalcomania—techniques guided by chance that any amateur could use. Breton considered the surrealist object—which Salvador Dalí defined as "an object [that] lends itself to a minimum of mechanical functions and is based on phantoms and representations liable to be provoked by the realization of unconscious acts"—to be "the concrete synthesis of [surrealism's] body of preoccupations." Dalí's "Lobster Telephone," Man Ray's "Gift" (a steam-iron embellished with a row of tacks protruding from its baseplate), and the magical landscapes-in-boxes Joseph Cornell fabricated out of bric-a-brac and photos of movie stars and ballerinas in his basement in Utopia Parkway in Queens, New York are well known examples of the genre. The most famous surrealist object of all is probably the "super-objective correlate of the female sex" over which (according to the surrealist painter Eileen Agar) T. S. Eliot long lingered at the 1936 International Surrealist Exhibition in London,

Meret Oppenheim's "Fur Lunch"—the fur-covered teacup, saucer, and spoon previously shown in *Fantastic Art, Dada, Surrealism*, which Alfred Barr described as "probably the most famous tea set in the world." Agar described herself as "Born in 1901 in Buenos Aires—reborn in the rue Schoelcher—has a foreign eye but an English finger and is Irish."

They pioneered installation art. Alyce Mahon argues that the transformations the surrealists wrought on Georges Wildenstein's Galérie Beaux-Arts for the 1938 Paris *Exposition internationale du surréalisme* threatened gender boundaries and all they had come to signify. Breton and Marcel Duchamp turned "the modernist 'white cube' gallery," she says, into "a space that was at once tactile and interactive as well as emphatically feminine," which "exposed repressed psychological anxiety and abandoned rationality (a male characteristic according to the western metaphysical tradition) and replaced it with irrationality and its feminine qualities (the insane, the primitive, subjective intuition, emotion and passion according to the same tradition)." Having entered the gallery through the infamous rue Surréaliste, a "vaginal" corridor lined with department-store mannequins dressed by the surrealists, viewers found themselves in a dim "uterine" chamber hung with 1200 coal sacks, containing a pool, a charcoal brazier and four large beds with satin sheets. Here paintings were exhibited to the smell of roasting coffee beans, the sound of hysterical laughter, and German marching music. On the opening night, wearing only a torn white dress that revealed as much as it concealed, the "surrealist dancer" and "Iris of mists" Helène Vanel performed what was described as an *acte manqué*, leaping on the beds and "gyrating, wailing and wrestling with a live rooster."

Looking back on the spectacle ten years (and a World War) later, Breton argued that the *Exposition internationale du surréalisme* was another manifestation of *hasard objectif.* Dismissed by critics at the time as gratuitously offensive, the installations in the Galérie Beaux-Arts in his view proved "only too premonitory, too portentous," for "we had stopped well short of the darkness and the underhanded cruelty of the coming days. We did not deliberately create that atmosphere: it merely conveyed the acute sense of foreboding with which we anticipated the coming decade." The surrealists, Breton insists, "had no other conscious intention in mind" than "creating an atmosphere as remote as possible from that of an 'art' gallery." But,

> by opening certain doors that rationalism boasted of having boarded up for good it may be that surrealism ... had enabled us here and there to make an excursion into the future, on condition that we should not be aware at the time that it was the future we were entering; that we should become aware of this and be able to make it evident only a posteriori.

Breton summarizes the fundamental principle underlying surrealism's experimental methods in his 1935 Prague lecture on the surrealist situation of the object. "The whole technical effort of Surrealism, from its very beginning up to the present day," he says, "has consisted in multiplying the ways to penetrate *the deepest layers of the mental.*" He goes on to quote Max Ernst, whose collages played "a decisive role ... in the creation of the particular view of things that we are here considering." Ernst regards the collage as the crystallization of surrealist epistemology:

I am tempted to consider this procedure [collage] to be the exploitation of *the fortuitous meeting of two distant realities on an inappropriate plane* (this is said as a paraphrase and a generalization of Lautreamont's famous phrase: "As beautiful as the fortuitous meeting of a sewing machine and an umbrella on an operating table," or, to use a shorter term, *the cultivation of the effects of a systematic bewildering*) ... A complete transmutation followed by a pure act such as love will necessarily be produced every time that the given facts—*the coupling of two realities which apparently cannot be coupled on a plane which apparently is not appropriate to them*—render conditions favorable.

Introducing Ernst's first Paris exhibition at the Au sans pareil bookstore in May-June 1921, Breton already identified "the marvelous ability to reach out, without leaving the field of our experience, to two distinct realities and bring them together to create a spark" as "what holds Dada's attention, for the time being." Milan Kundera sees such juxtapositions as the key to "breaking through the plausibility barrier ... Not in order to escape the real world (the way the Romantics did) but to apprehend it better." Discussing Franz Kafka's novels—which he thinks achieved the "fusion of dream and reality" Breton called for in the *Manifesto of Surrealism* a decade before it was written—Kundera also invokes "Lautréamont's [phrase] about the beauty in the chance encounter between an umbrella and a sewing machine: the more alien things are from one another, the more magical the light that spring from their contact. I'd like to call it a poetics of surprise," he goes on; "or beauty as perpetual astonishment. Or to use the notion of *density* as a criterion of value: density of imagination, density of unexpected encounters." Such density would be no bad criterion of value for the sociological imagination, too.

4
The Photographic Uncanny

Of all surrealism's modes of systematic bewildering the camera proved perhaps its most potent instrument for uncovering the marvelous in the mundane. Like many avant-garde interwar photographers the surrealists experimented with photograms, photomontages, and multiple exposures in search of a new vision. Lee Miller (re)discovered solarization by pure serendipity: when a mouse ran over her foot in Man Ray's darkroom she briefly turned on the light, causing a halo effect in negatives that were in the developing tank. Susan Sontag dismisses much of this experimentation as contrived and passé—a position, I would suggest, which is itself beginning to look somewhat dated in the wake of wider reevaluations of the surrealist legacy. The context for this dismissal, however, is a more general argument with which I concur. "The error of the surrealist militants," Sontag thinks, "was to imagine the surreal as something universal, that is, a matter of psychology, whereas it turns out to be *what is most local, ethnic, class-bound, dated.*" In his defense Breton did recognize that

> The marvelous is not the same in every period of history: it partakes in some obscure way of a sort of general revelation only the fragments of which come down to us: they are the romantic *ruins*, the modern *mannequin*, or any other symbol capable of affecting the human sensibility for a period of time.

"Mind" is never just a matter of individual psychology. Breton's "deepest layers of the mental" are always already social, which is also to say historical. As Walter Benjamin might have said, nothing dates an era like its dreams.

For this reason, Sontag argues, photography is "the one art that has managed to carry out ... a Surrealist takeover of the modern sensibility." Photography is never more surrealist than when it is at its most documentary. And surrealism "lies at the very heart of the photographic enterprise, in the creation of a duplicate world, of a reality in the second degree." The Czech surrealist Jindřich Štyrský's images of the assorted masks, coffins, prostheses, busts, musical boxes, palmists' charts, and fallen angels in Bohemian shop windows are excellent examples of what might be called the straight photography of the uncanny. So too are Lee Miller's photographs of London during the Blitz, published in 1941 as *Grim Glory: Pictures of Britain Under Fire.* Her images include "Revenge on Culture" (a fallen female nude statue, covered in rubble, her throat slashed by what looks like a stray cable), "Bridge of Sighs" (what is left of an upper story connecting two terraced houses above a yawning gap where a third had once stood), and "Remington

Silent" (a pulverized typewriter, its keys twisted this way and that). Miller followed the Allied armies from Normandy to Berlin as a war correspondent for *Vogue*, where her photos of "grim skeletal corpses from Buchenwald" were "separated by a few thicknesses of paper from delightful recipes to be prepared by beautiful women dressed in sumptuous gowns." There can be few denser unexpected encounters or more graphic illustrations of the revelatory power of distant realities meeting by chance on an apparently inappropriate plane. "Being a Surrealist artist," comments Miller's son Antony Penrose, "must be the only possible training to enable a person to retain their objectivity in the face of the total illogicality of War." As Breton always insisted, it is reality itself that is surreal.

Reminding us that "surrealism has always courted accidents, welcomed the uninvited, flattered disorderly presences," Sontag points out that photographs "don't seem deeply beholden to the intentions of the artist, but owe their existence to a loose cooperation (quasi-magical, quasi-accidental) between photographer and subject—mediated by an ever simpler and more automated machine." In a perfect synthesis of Breton's magical-circumstantial and exploding-fixed the photographic image fixes Henri Cartier-Bresson's "decisive moment" for eternity. Might we go so far as to say that there is a sense in which every photograph petrifies coincidence—the same sense in which, for Roland Barthes, in photographs "there is always a defeat of Time," an intimation of a death to come? The English surrealist and documentary filmmaker Humphrey Jennings thought so. He accepts that "photography itself—'photogenic drawing'—began simply as the mechanisation of realism, and it remains *the* system with which the people can be pictured by the people for the people: simple to operate, results capable of mass reproduction and circulation, effects generally considered truthful ('the camera cannot lie'), and so on." But Jennings, too, finds something distinctly surreal in the photographic image, which he interprets in Freudian terms:

> intellectually the importance of the camera lies clearly in the way in which it deals with problems of choice—choice and avoidance of choice. Freud ("Psychopathology of Everyday Life" p. 203) says that the feeling of *Déja Vu* ("Who does that remind you of?") "corresponds to the memory of an unconscious fantasy." The camera is precisely an instrument for recording the object or image that prompted that memory. Hence the rush to see "how they came out."

"In the same book," he drily adds, "Freud insists on the impossibility of a voluntarily 'arbitrary' choice or association of objects."

Fundamental to the photographic uncanny is the presence of absence, the eternal return of *what once was*. Ripped out of the contexts of its own times and spaces, what habitually passes below the radar of consciousness is rendered freshly visible as *image*. The camera accomplishes the same displacement as Marcel Duchamp's readymades, forcing us to look at the familiar through different eyes. For Sontag, the "earliest surrealist photographs" date from the 1850s,

> when photographers first went out prowling the streets of London, Paris and New York, looking for their unposed slice of life. These photographs— *concrete, particular, anecdotal* (except that the anecdote has been effaced)—moments of lost time,

of vanished customs—seem far more surreal to us now than any photograph rendered abstract and poetic by superimposition, under-printing, solarization, and the like.

A true genealogy of surrealist photography would extend through Paul Martin's London and Arnold Genthe's San Francisco Chinatown in the 1890s through Atget's "twilight Paris of shabby streets and decaying trades" (which the surrealists loved) and "the dramas of sex and loneliness depicted in Brassaï's *Paris de nuit*" to "the image of the city as a theater of disaster in Weegee's *Naked City*." We might want to add to that list Robert Frank's "deliberately random" *The Americans*, Bill Owens's *Suburbia*, William Eggleston's *Democratic Forest*, Daido Moriyama's *Shinjuku*, Martin Parr's *The Last Resort*, and Alec Soth's *Songbook*—and much else. "I think people like the book because it shows what people think about but don't discuss," Robert Frank says of *The Americans*. "*It shows what's on the edge of their mind.*" He was searching less for Henri Cartier-Bresson's decisive moment than "some moment I couldn't explain."

Roland Barthes begins *Camera Lucida* with "an amazement I have not been able to lessen since" at the realization, upon looking at an 1852 photograph of Napoleon's younger brother Jerome, that "I am looking at eyes that once looked at the Emperor." He was not looking at any such *thing*, of course; he was only looking at an *image*. But a trace of Jerome was nonetheless there in the photograph in a way it would not have been in a painting or drawing. The source of Barthes' amazement—and the reason for the power of the photograph, as distinct from any other visual image—is this:

In the Photograph, the event is never transcended for the sake of something else: the Photograph ... is the absolute Particular, the sovereign Contingency, matte and somehow stupid, the This ... in short, what Lacan calls the *Tuché*, the Occasion, the Encounter, the Real, in its indefatigable expression.

Unlike other visual representations (but like phonograph recordings) the photograph is not an attempted replica of the real but an object that bears its direct imprint. It carries into the world of language the material trace of what language supplants, muddying the boundary between the world of signs and the world of things. "It is as if the Photograph always carries its referent with itself, both affected by the same amorous or funereal immobility, at the very heart of the world," Barthes writes. And "This fatality (no photograph without *something* or *someone*) involves Photography in the vast disorder of objects—of all the objects in the world." A photograph is always two-faced: a message, a part of the world of signs, capable of entering many signifying chains and conveying as many meanings, but at the same time a physical object, a dumb emissary from the ineffable Lacanian real, which insistently drags us back to the world beyond language. If Milan Kundera is correct, that world is one that is always irreparably lost, at least as a possible object of knowledge:

We know reality only in the past tense. We do not know it as it is in the present, in the moment when it's happening, when it is. The present moment is unlike the memory of it. Remembering is not the negative of forgetting. Remembering is a form of forgetting ... The present—the concreteness of the present—as a phenomenon to consider, as a structure, is for us an unknown planet; so that we can neither hold on to it in our memory nor reconstruct it through imagination. We die without knowing what we have lived.

Craig Campbell builds upon Barthes' insight to suggest that the most useful role for photographs in the social sciences may be to act as "*agents provocateurs* within institutional archives." "Photographs," he suggests, "consistently threaten meaningful narratives that they are often employed to illustrate," functioning "as documents of witness and presence [that] drive a critique of mundane particularity into fields of representation which so often efface the everyday and the ordinary." The objects that went off to dream at Campbell's antique fair were thousands of glass-plate negatives from Soviet cultural-construction projects among the indigenous peoples of Siberia, all marked by manipulation, damage, and degradation. Campbell is "attracted to these imperfections," he says, because "they point to a fissure in an otherwise closed system of representation," upsetting "the clean and arrogant historiography that claims to tell you everything that you need to know." The plates expose "the public secret that the relationship between the historian and the past is as much an art as a science in its reliance on serendipity, creativity, selective vision, and accident." Though Campbell's negatives "document ... the late Russian Imperial era, the Communist revolution of 1917, and subsequent decades of Communist development and social construction projects," they "fail to *capture* all this." Each negative points beneath and beyond the narratives in which we have named events and ordered them into histories to "the dense and particular wealth of ordinary life; the irreducibly deep and strange, the impossibly complex dynamism of humans, plants, animals, projects, aspirations, weather, obligations; life as it is lived, not as it is written."

Every one of Campbell's glass plates is a "relentless indication of specificity," a *punctum* that may blow apart the *studium* through which we make history legible. Campbell argues that the "ashes and dust" that have degraded the negatives must be permitted "to opportunistically trail our interpretive works, to dirty up the history, to debase the narrative," operating as "a contagion of entropy, terrorizing the myth of order produced in the archive. The formlessness of the everyday is the agency behind photography's agitation." He is employing the concept of *informe* (formlessness) here advanced by Georges Bataille in 1929 as "a term serving to declassify [*déclasser*]"—another and very potent way of making trouble. Back in 1916 Breton had been attracted to the same quality in the nihilistic wounded infantry officer Jacques Vaché, "whose influence touched me to the core ... in Vaché's person, in utmost secrecy, a principle of total insubordination was undermining the world, reducing everything that then seemed all-important to a petty scale, desecrating everything in its path." Bataille's target was "academics" who want to shoehorn "what exists into a frock-coat, a mathematical frock-coat." "Formlessness," Campbell concludes, "is informed by the task of *bringing things 'down in the world'* [Bataille]. The photograph as archive of the everyday presents not order but its opposite, evidence of disorder and disarray."

5
The Ethnographic Surreal

James Clifford follows Susan Sontag in understanding surrealism as "a pervasive—perhaps dominant—modern *sensibility*," which he characterizes as "an aesthetic that values *fragments, curious collections, unexpected juxtapositions*—that works to provoke the manifestation of extraordinary realities drawn from the domains of the erotic, the exotic, and the unconscious." One virtue of this approach is that the compass of the term is broadened beyond the official surrealist group around André Breton to include so-called dissident surrealists like Bataille, Robert Desnos, and André Masson, with whom Breton settled accounts in the *Second Manifesto of Surrealism*. The manifesto was published in December 1929 in the final issue of *La Révolution Surréaliste*, surmounted by red lipstick kisses. The heretics responded the following month with the pamphlet *A Corpse*, which depicted Breton on its cover as Christ crowned with thorns and mocked him as "a great big soft strumpet armed with a gift-wrapped library of dreams." Describing himself as "surrealism's old enemy *from within*," Bataille accused Breton of reducing the unconscious to "no more than a pitiable treasure-trove" (and emasculating the Marquis de Sade).

Together with Carl Einstein, the author of the earliest book on African art *Negerplastik* (*Black Sculpture*, 1915) and Georges Henri Rivière, deputy director of the Museum of Ethnography at the Trocadéro, Bataille's group formed the core of the review *Documents* (1929-30), which proclaimed its interests as "*Archéologie—Beaux-Arts—Ethnographie—Variétés.*" Back in the days of the Bureau for Surrealist Research Antonin Artaud (who took over direction of the Bureau in January 1925 at Breton's behest) had charged Bataille's close collaborator Michel Leiris with compiling a "Glossary of the Marvelous and a Directory of Surrealist Ideas." Leiris described *Documents* as "a Janus-faced publication with one side turned towards the higher spheres of culture ... and the other towards a savage domain where travellers ventured with neither map nor passport of any kind." He does not specify where the latter domain lies, but in *Documents'* pages Ekoi ritual dance masks keep company with the Marquis de Sade's handwriting, Stravinsky's *Capriccio*, and the Fox Movietone Follies of 1929, while Eddie South and his Alabamians and the Hayman Swayze Plantation Orchestra rub shoulders with "André Masson: the Universal Dismemberer," the art of the Solomon Islands, and Sacheverell Sitwell on the Mexican baroque. According to Clifford, "The journal's basic method is juxtaposition—fortuitous or ironic collage," in which the proper arrangement of cultural symbols and artifacts is constantly placed in doubt [...] Its images, in their equalizing gloss and distancing effect, present in the same plane a Châtelet show advertisement, a Hollywood movie clip, a Picasso, a Giacometti, a documentary photo from colonial New Caledonia, a newspaper clip, an Eskimo mask, an Old Master, a musical instrument.

This is a systematic deployment of Ernst's collage principle in the service of a radical cultural leveling—a *déclassement*.

Documents' "Critical Dictionary," a heterotopic glossary that ran from issue to issue, included articles on Dust, Eye, Factory Chimney, Kali, (Buster) Keaton, Man, Materialism, Metamorphosis, Skyscraper, and Talkie. Bataille wrote more than half the entries himself; the next most prolific contributor was Leiris. In "Architecture" ("it is in the form of cathedrals and palaces that Church and State speak to and impose silence upon the crowds") Bataille pens the acid aphorism "man would seem to represent merely an intermediary stage within the morphological development between monkey and building." It is a formulation that would have delighted Michel Foucault and other later undoers of the Cartesian subject. "Museum" and "Slaughterhouse" scandalously couple realities that apparently cannot be coupled on a plane that apparently is not appropriate to them. Noting that the first public museum collection was inaugurated "on 27 July 1793, in France, by the Convention," Bataille sardonically observes: "The origin of the modern museum would thus be linked to the development of the guillotine."

Bataille sees the slaughterhouse as "linked to religion in that the temples of bygone eras ... served two purposes: they were used both for prayer and killing.

The result (and this judgment is confirmed by the chaotic aspect of present-day slaughterhouses) was certainly a disturbing convergence of the mysteries of myth and the ominous grandeur typical of those places in which blood flows." The entry is illustrated by Elie Lotar's photographs of the abattoir at La Villette, the most famous of which shows a row of severed hocks and hooves neatly lined up along the base of a wall. Bataille was not the first to couple the sacred and the slaughter-house. Here is the British poet Wilfred Owen, writing in the trenches on the Western Front sometime between 8 October 1917 and his death in March, 1918:

> If in some smothering dreams you too could pace
> Behind the wagon that we flung him in,
> And watch the white eyes writhing in his face,
> His hanging face, like a devil's sick of sin;
> If you could hear, at every jolt, the blood
> Come gargling from the froth-corrupted lungs,
> Obscene as cancer, bitter as the cud
> Of vile, incurable sores on innocent tongues,
> My friend, you would not tell with such high zest
> To children ardent for some desperate glory,
> The old Lie; Dulce et Decorum est
>   Pro patria mori.

Although there had been plentiful earlier inti-mations of a cultural crisis of modernity (Baudelaire, Rimbaud, Lautréamont, Cézanne, the cubists), for Clifford it was above all the slaughterhouse—or should we perhaps say, the colossal ritual *sacrifice?*—of World War I that cut the modern self "loose from its attach-ments" to "discover meaning where it may—a predica-ment, evoked at its most nihilistic, that underlies both surrealism and modern ethnography." Max Ernst would have agreed: "On the first of August 1914," he writes in a set of autobiographical notes whose constant revisions (knowingly) undermine the very notion of a stable subject, "M. E. died. He was resurrected on the eleventh of November 1914 as a young man who aspired to find the myths of his time." The war was a decisive formative experience for the surrealist generation: around the time that Breton was pondering the ravings of the shell-shocked at the military hospital at Saint-Dizier where he served in 1917 as a medical orderly, at Verdun "The German gunner, Max Ernst, was bombarding the trenches where I, a French infantryman, was on the lookout. Three years later, we were the best of friends"—reminisced Paul Éluard in "Poetic Evidence." "For us," Ernst later explained, Dada

> resulted from the absurdity, the whole immense stupidity, of that imbecilic war. We young people had come back from the war in a state of stupefaction, and our rage had to find expression somehow or other. This it did quite naturally through *attacks on the foundations of the civilization* responsible for the war. Attacks on speech, syntax, logic, literature, painting and so on.

After the war, Clifford maintains, "the world was permanently surrealist." There were no more truths universally acknowledged. Nothing—least of all the foundations of western civilization—could be taken to be self-evident any more. It was a moment of estrangement in which "Culture and its norms (beauty, truth, reality)" became visible as "artificial arrangements susceptible to detached analysis and comparison with other possible dispositions," for which "Africa (and to a lesser degree Oceana and America) provided a reservoir of other forms and other beliefs." Clifford insists that this openness to "the other (whether accessible in dreams, fetishes, or Lévy-Bruhl's *mentalité primitive*)" is a fundamentally different phenomenon from the voyeuristic exoticism of the nineteenth century. Where the latter "departed from a more-or-less confident cultural order in search of a temporary *frisson*,"

> Modern ethnography and surrealism began with a reality deeply in question. Others appeared now as serious human alternatives; modern cultural relativism became possible ... For every local custom or truth there was always an exotic alternative, a possible juxtaposition or incongruity. Below (psychologically) and beyond (geographically) ordinary reality there existed another reality. Surrealism shared this ironic situation with relativist ethnography.

The "modern cultural situation" is one "generated by a continual play of the familiar and the strange, of which ethnography and surrealism are two elements." While "the ethnographic label suggests a characteristic attitude of participant observation among the artifacts of a defamiliarized cultural reality," the surrealist attitude "tended to work in the reverse sense, *making the familiar strange*."

Claude Lévi-Strauss drew a similar parallel in a series of lectures he delivered in Tokyo in 1986. "To know and understand one's own culture," he argues, "it is necessary to regard it from the point of view of another. This can be likened to the Noh actor as described by [the] great [Japanese] playwright and theorist Zeami: to judge his performance, the actor must learn to see himself as if he was the spectator." This shift of perspective, he also says, "could be called *a technique of 'making strange'*":

Anthropologists exist to attest that the way we live, the values we believe in, are not the only ones possible, that other ways of life, other systems of values have allowed and continue to allow human communities to find happiness. Anthropology invites us therefore to temper our misplaced vanity, to respect other ways of life, to call ourselves into question through knowledge of other customs that astonish us, shock us, or repel us—somewhat like Jean-Jacques Rousseau, who preferred to believe that gorillas, recently described by the travelers of his time, were men, rather than run the risk of denying the humanity of beings who, perhaps, revealed an as-yet unknown aspect of human nature.

Ethnography and surrealism provided complementary disorientations—or symmetrical displacements—that offered alternative standpoints from which to begin to critique the given order of things.

Breton and Bataille later cooperated on *Minotaure* (1933-9), a sumptuously illustrated magazine published by Albert Skira that aimed to "rediscover, reunite and resume the elements that have constituted the modern movement." At the start *Minotaure* embraced ethnography, archaeology, the history of religion, mythology, and psychoanalysis alongside the arts. Jacques Lacan was among the contributors to the first issue. The second was entirely devoted to Marcel Griaule's ethnographic expedition from Dakar to Djibouti—a journey across sub-Saharan Africa lasting two years, of which Michel Leiris was the recording secretary. Leiris published his diaries from the exhibition in 1934 as *L'Afrique fantôme*. *Minotaure* was eventually taken over by Breton's group and became more of a surrealist art review, albeit (in the judgment of the Hungarian photographer Brassaï, who had no great love for Breton) "the best art review in the world, containing in germ, or already in flower, everything that burst forth in art, poetry or literature twenty or thirty years later." In 1937 Bataille and Leiris teamed up with Roger Caillois, another ex-surrealist who had fallen out with Breton (over the great man's refusal to cut open a Mexican jumping bean because it might destroy the "mystery" within), to found the Collège de Sociologie. The project of the Collège—further exemplifying Clifford's argument of the breaking down of presumed barriers between modern western selves and primitive others—was to produce a "sacred sociology of the contemporary world."

In *Man and the Sacred*, published in 1939, Caillois took up Max Ernst's quest for the myths of a time that prided itself on having turned its enlightened scientific back on myths. "Myth will be found," he insists, "even where it is at first regarded as repugnant, as soon as one seeks it in its proper milieu." He asks what in the modern world has replaced the "exhausting and ruinous festivals" that punctuated the life of "civilizations described as primitive"—festivals that he, like Émile Durkheim before him, regarded as the paradoxical guarantors of social cohesion. By the time a second edition of the book came out in 1949 Caillois had abundant evidence to support his unpalatable answer. "The primitive festival," he reminds his readers, "is a time of excess":

> Reserves accumulated over the course of several years are squandered. The holiest laws are violated, those that seem at the very basis of social life. Yesterday's crime is now prescribed, and in place of customary rules, new taboos and disciplines are established, the purpose of which is not to avoid or

soothe intense emotions, but rather to excite and bring them to climax ... This fervor is also the time for sacrifices, even the time for the sacred, a time outside of time that recreates, purifies and rejuvenates society ...

"One can scarcely find in complex and machine civilizations a single equivalent of this crisis that cuts so brutally into the monotonous heart of daily life that is so extremely in contrast to it," he goes on. There is "only one phenomenon [that] manifests comparable importance, intensity, and explosiveness, of the same order of grandeur—*war*."

6
An Insurrection Against History

Whatever their differences with Bataille and his circle, Breton and his friends were not afraid to name the given order of things not only as modern and bourgeois but also as white, western, and—rather more belatedly and in ways that remain contentious—male, pointing to the intimate linkages between modalities of knowledge and embodiments of power. A voyage around the world in 1924 left Paul Éluard disgusted at "the imbecilic cruelties of white decadence." "In Indonesia," he wrote in "The Abolition of Slavery," published the following year in *La Révolution Surréaliste*, "the white man is no more than a corpse, and this corpse throws his shit in the faces of people with yellow skin." In their tract opposing the Moroccan War the surrealists proclaimed their "absolute detachment ... from the ideas which are at the base of European civilization," declaring "*an insurrection against History.*" It was this campaign that first brought them into the orbit of the French

Communist Party, which Breton and several other members of the Paris surrealist group joined in 1927 (only, in Breton and Éluard's case, to be expelled in 1933). Three decades later "André Breton, surrealist" was prominent among the signatories of the "Manifesto of the 121," published in *Vérité-Liberté* on 6 September 1960 (and immediately seized by the police), which called for the French public to recognize the Algerian War as a legitimate struggle for independence.

The surrealists were vociferous critics of the International Colonial Exhibition of 1931, held in Paris to showcase the products of French and other European colonies (the United Kingdom, which had put its own overseas possessions on display at the British Empire Exhibition at Wembley in 1924, was a conspicuous absentee). Among the many exotic attractions on show in the Bois de Vincennes was a replica of the principal temple at Angkor Wat in Cambodia, which was then part of French Indochina. The spectacle lasted six months, attracting an estimated eight million visitors to the city. The surrealists called for a boycott and contributed to a Comintern-sponsored counter-exhibition *The Truth about the Colonies*, which was appropriately staged in the constructivist Soviet pavilion the Vesnin brothers had created for the Art Deco exhibition of 1925. Alongside exhibits on colonial conquest and forced labor was a hall designed by Yves Tanguy presenting artifacts from Africa, Oceana, and America taken from the personal collections of Breton, Éluard, and Tristan Tzara. In another formless equalizing plane these "were offset ... by the fetishes of the West: Christian objects, objects of worship in the vein of Saint-Sulpice, and so on."

The surrealists' description of these objects as "idols from the world over" in their leaflet "A First

Evaluation of the Colonial Exhibition" nicely illustrates Clifford's thesis. "Just as the adversaries of nationalisms must defend the nationalism of oppressed peoples, the adversaries of art that is the fruit of the capitalist economy must dialectically oppose to it the art of oppressed peoples," they went on to explain. What occasioned this outburst was the burning down of the Dutch East Indies pavilion at the Colonial Exhibition, which had destroyed the "most precious testimonies of intellectual life in Malaysia and Melanesia ... objects that have been taken violently from those who had conceived them." While the fire might have started accidentally the surrealists saw it as another instance of *hasard objectif*, a subconscious "*acte manqué*" on behalf of Christian missionaries who "habitually mutilate fetishes and ... drill the indigenous peoples in their schools to reproduce the traits of their Christ according to the most banal recipes of European art." "This is how the *work of colonization* is carried out," they thundered, "a work which began with massacres, and has continued through conversions, forced labor and disease."

Breton's own firsthand acquaintance with the non-European world began with a journey to Mexico in 1938 where he hung out with Diego Rivera and Frida Kahlo, co-authored a manifesto "For an Independent Revolutionary Art" with the exiled Leon Trotsky, and collected gaily-colored devotional pictures and other artifacts of popular culture to add to the *Wunderkammer* that was his apartment at 42 rue Fontaine in the seedy Paris quarter of Pigalle. He escaped Vichy France in March 1941 with his second wife Jacqueline Lamba and their five-year-old daughter Aube on a ship out of Marseille bound for Martinique full of "Germans, Austrians, Czechs, Spaniards, and a handful of French ... fleeing barbaric racial prejudice" or "just paying for the crime of holding noble ideals under the noses of their present masters." Life on board the *Capitaine Paul-Lemerle*, he writes, was "uncomfortable, precarious, and uselessly odious." Breton's fellow-passengers included the writer Victor Serge, the Cuban surrealist painter Wifredo Lam, and Claude Lèvi-Strauss. "We were to become firm friends in the course of an exchange of letters which we kept up through our interminable journey," the great anthropologist relates; "their subject was the relation between aesthetic beauty and originality." What else? On arrival in France *outre-mer* Breton was thankful that "the thin dormitory pallet has been folded away for the last time" and "the people in charge of the slaughtering and butchering the sheep and cattle will no longer put on their midafternoon show on this deck in the way they did, surrounded by a large audience of children." An image lingered in his mind of "three objects lined up in a row and entwining their flames—a disemboweled cow hanging from the day before, the cabins on the afterdeck, and the rising sun."

On disembarking at Fort-de-France Breton found himself interned in the one-time leper colony of Lazaret, which was now the concentration camp of Point-Rouge. He was released after a week but his movements were shadowed by secret police throughout the seventeen days he spent on the island. Buying a ribbon for Aube in a variety store, he chanced upon the first issue of a magazine called *Tropiques*. He could not believe his eyes: "what was said was just what needed to be said, not only well, but as forcefully as one could say it! All those grimacing shadows were shredded and dispersed ... Aimé Césaire was the name of the one who spoke." "By one of those chance happenings that reveal privileged moments" the woman who ran the store turned out to be the sister of Réné Ménil, Césaire's collaborator on *Tropiques*. "And the next day, Césaire. I can recall my initial response in discovering his pure blackness," Breton confesses, "something I did not notice at first because of his smile." Césaire's "appearance in his own element—and I do not mean only on that day—takes on the significance of *a sign of the times*":

> a black man who handles the French language as no white man today is capable of handling it. And it is a black man who is the one guiding us today into the unexplored, seeming to play as he goes, throwing ignition switches that lead us forward from spark to spark. And it is a black man who, not only for blacks but for all humankind, expresses all the questions, all the anguish, all the hopes and all the ecstasy and who becomes more and more crucial as the supreme example of dignity.

The two poets met up several times more before Breton left. For his part, Césaire later recalled this encounter as "utterly crucial and decisive ... If I am who I am today, I believe that much of it is due to my meeting with André Breton. [It was like] a great short-cut toward finding myself."

By the time Breton returned to France in May 1946 exile (in New York), travel (to Canada, the American West, Haiti, and the Dominican Republic), and new acquaintances—including his Chilean third wife Elisa Claro, whom he met in a 56th Street restaurant in Manhattan in 1943 after breaking up with Jacqueline—had greatly expanded his cultural horizons. "From America," records Jean Schuster, he returned with splendors: agates from Gaspesia, Elisa, Hopi and Zuni kachinas, the complete works of Charles Fourier, Aube promised to *l'amour fou*, masks from the Pacific Northwest, the friendship of Claude Lévi-Strauss, Robert Lebel, and Georges Duthuit, the magic of his stay in the Antilles and his meetings with Aimé Césaire, Magloire Saint-Aude, Hyppolite.

Breton wrote *Arcanum 17* in the Gaspé Peninsula in Quebec, where he vacationed with Elisa during the fall of 1944. The text is an extraordinary poetic *dérive* through love, war, liberty, alchemy, the convulsive beauty of the Canadian landscape, French historiography, the myth of Messalina, the "black god" Osiris, and above all the potentialities of "magical" thought to liberate the human spirit from its modern shackles of an all-consuming rationality. "Who today could deny the radical power of surrealism?" asked Georges Bataille, reviewing *Arcanum 17* in 1946 for *Critique*.

Echoing Max Ernst's rejection of "the foundations of the civilization responsible for the war"—the previous war, the supposed Great War to end wars—*Arcanum 17* castigates "all the types of reasoning which men are so shabbily proud of, which they're so miserably duped by." "This crisis is so severe," Breton proclaims,

> that I, myself, see only one solution: the time has come to value the ideas of women at the expense of those of man, whose bankruptcy is coming to pass fairly tumultuously today ... Rémy de Gourmant will be paid back for his insult to Rimbaud: "A girl's temperament," said he. Today, a judgment of this sort shows us the measure of he who made it: it tells us all we need to build a case against *the male type of*

intelligence at the end of the nineteenth century ... Let art yield the passing lane to the supposedly 'irrational' feminine, let it fiercely make enemies of all that which, having the effrontery to present itself as sure and solid, bears in reality the mark of that masculine intransigence which, in the field of human relations at the international level, shows well enough today what it is capable of ...

Simone Breton, who on 7 January 1925 had recorded her protest in the *Cahier de la permanence* at the Bureau of Surrealist Research against "the procedures employed with certain female members who are charged with handling certain chores and [are] treated like instruments," might have smiled.

7
Savage Civilization

On the other side of the English Channel the unlikely trio of Tom Harrisson, Charles Madge, and Humphrey Jennings were meantime setting up an idiosyncratic anthropological enterprise of their own that perfectly exemplifies Clifford's confluence of surrealism and ethnography. These men did not enjoy university positions and were not popular with the academic establishment of the day. Imperial misfits born abroad and abandoned to the surrealities of an English boarding school education, Harrisson and Madge became Cambridge dropouts. Jennings had better luck, taking a first in English at Pembroke College in 1929. Madge and Jennings met as students and stayed good friends. A poet who published his first collection *The Disappearing Castle* with Faber in 1937, Madge worked for a time for the *Daily Mirror*. "Fourteen months as a reporter," he later wrote, "taught me to understand the queer poetry of the newspaper and the advertisement hoarding," which "serve as vehicles for the expression of unconscious fears and wishes of the mass." He instanced "the *Daily Mirror* headline which astonished London on December 3, 1936: THE KING WANTS TO MARRY MRS. SIMPSON: CABINET ADVISES 'NO'"—in which, he believed, "millions saw the emergence of their own thwarted and concealed desires." Jennings cut his professional teeth working for John Grierson's General Post Office Film Unit, which was based near the home Madge shared with his fellow-poet Kathleen Raine in the London suburb of Blackheath. He would become one of Britain's most renowned documentary filmmakers.

Madge and Jennings were both deeply involved with the British wing of the surrealist movement. Michel Remy's *Surrealism in Britain* credits Madge with writing "the first thoroughgoing article on the specificity of English surrealism," published in *New Verse* in 1933—a little magazine (its editors boasted) that could "be bought for sixpence—the price of ten Players [cigarettes] or a brief library borrowing of *Angel Pavement* or a 'bus fare from Piccadilly Circus to Golders Green." Like Paul Éluard, Madge believed that "surrealism is not a literary school" but "a laboratory of studies, of experimentation, that rejects all inclinations of individualism." "One cannot treat surrealist poetry separately from the other activities of the surrealist laboratory," he insisted. Madge was a somewhat desultory member of the Communist Party, which he joined in 1932. His 1936 prose-poem "Bourgeois News" offers an apocalyptic vision of a Britain in which "Floods are frequent because the rivers ... have been neglected for a century":

The mountains heaved up like a rough sea for twelve miles, and the hamlet with its 200 inhabitants disappeared. Two mailcoaches arrived safely at their destination, but with the drivers frozen dead in their seats. Trains were buried for three days. London awoke to chaos on the 19th. The snow lay a uniform solid three feet thick and fifteen feet in drifts. Many boats careered wildly along the road, crashing into houses and other buildings on the river bank. The crew of the Strathrye soaked their beds in paraffin and ignited them to attract attention. Days were passed in making shrouds, in farewells, in drinking holy thin soup. The schools were empty so that the whole family could die together, and no debts were paid.

Jennings was on the organizing committee for the 1936 London International Surrealist Exhibition, where he personally exhibited six items, one of them a satirical collage featuring Lord Kitchener titled *Minotaur*. He helped stage *The Impact of Machines* exhibition at the surrealists' London Gallery in Cork Street in April 1938 and had a solo exhibition there later the same year. He was deputy editor of the British surrealist journal *London Bulletin* (1938-40) and co-translated Benjamin Péret's *Remove Your Hat* with the poet David Gascoyne, author of one of the earliest (and best) books on surrealism in English. Paul Éluard's prefatory note commends *Remove Your Hat* for its "major accent, eternal and modern, which explodes and leaves a gaping hole in a world of prudently ordained necessities and murmured fairy-stories." Gascoyne was another who "joined the Communist Party as one did in those days." Jennings, too, believed in a socially engaged surrealism, reminding Herbert Read and Hugh Sykes-Davies (whom he accused of co-opting surrealism for literary romanticism) that

"Coincidences" have the infinite freedom of appearing anywhere, anytime, to anyone: in broad daylight to those whom we most despise in places we have most loathed: not even to us at all: probably least to petty seekers after mystery and poetry on deserted sea-shores and in misty junk-shops.

The same text contrasted "the mixed atmosphere of cultural hysteria and amateur theatricality which combined to make the [London] Surrealist Exhibition of June such a 'success'" with "the passion terror and excitement, dictated by absolute integrity and produced with all the poetry of bare necessity, which emanated from *La Révolution Surréaliste*." A few years later Jennings's surrealist sensibility would serve him exactly as Lee Miller's did when she shot the images for *Grim Glory*. It is May 1941, and we are a long way from deserted seashores and misty junkshops —but not a million miles from Charles Madge's chaotic imaginings in "Bourgeois News":

I see a thousand strange sights in the streets of
   London
I see the clock on Bow Church burning in daytime
I see a one-legged man crossing the fire on
   crutches
I see three negroes and a woman with white face-
   powder reading music at half-past three in the
   morning
I see an ambulance girl with her arms full of roses
I see the burnt drums of the Philharmonic
I see the green leaves of Lincolnshire carried
   through London on the wrecked body of an
   aircraft

Tom Harrisson had no such artistic or literary associations. As a self-taught ornithologist at Harrow

School, at the age of eighteen he enlisted 1300 observers to take part in the first UK national census of the Great Crested Grebe—an inquiry into "a little known matter of great importance" that continues to this day. "In order to assure the maximum of response," Harrison explained,

> appeals for help were published in daily, evening and local newspapers, weekly and sporting papers, angling and scientific journals, and a special feature in *The Times*. The B.B.C. kindly broadcast an appeal at the beginning of the general news, while *British Birds*, *The Scottish Naturalist* and *The Naturalist* published special articles on our behalf. We wrote personally to every well-known naturalist and ornithologist, to many local observers, taxidermists, town clerks and clergy with lakes in their parishes; we circulated a great number of landowners with likely lakes on their property; and we did every other conceivable thing to make the enquiry a truly national one.

"Landowners in every part of the country gave invaluable assistance," Harrison and Hollom's report continues, which was "often detailed and *more accurate than that supplied by ornithologists.* Keepers and agents were also very helpful, and not one case of erroneous identification was discovered. A mass of supplementary data was obtained, much of it valuable."

It was on an ornithological expedition to Sarawak in 1932 that Harrisson "found, for once, that he liked and was liked immediately by a group of people, the longhouse dwellers of north-central Borneo." "Ever after," claims the *Dictionary of National Biography*, "he fitted in better with 'primitive' people abroad and with working-class people in

England than with members of his own class." Birdwatching slipped into people watching when Harrisson joined an Oxford University ethnographic exhibition to the New Hebrides in July 1933 and stayed on among the cannibals of Malekula when the expedition officially ended in early 1934. Eventually, he writes, the joint British-French colonial administration "decided that it was worth employing me, as acting district agent for six months, while the permanent agent had a break from the view off his east coasts verandah." Harrisson was "brought back to civilization" (the DNB continues) in November 1935 "by none other than Douglas Fairbanks (Sr), who called with a yacht and signed him up as adviser for a Hollywood movie." In 1936 he moved to Bolton in industrial Lancashire where he went deep undercover as a truck driver, ice-cream vendor and shop assistant, surreptitiously taking notes on the people around him.

Harrisson vigorously defended the cannibals' way of life in *Savage Civilisation*, which was published by the left-wing house of Victor Gollancz in 1937 and became a popular bestseller. The book begins with an attempt at "an outline of tribal life in north-west Malekula ... the necessary foundation to the story." But thereafter Harrisson sets his encounter with the "savages" within the long history of attempted white civilization of the New Hebrides that began with Pedro Fernandez de Quiros' landfall while in search of Terra Australis in 1606, proceeded fitfully through exploratory visits from la Perouse, Cook, and Bligh, and took off in earnest with the discovery in 1828 of sandalwood, whose perfume was highly prized in China. During the "period of vigorous and vicious exploitation" that followed, *"savage comes into its own."* Harrisson is speaking here of "the strong-arm element of European civilization." Demand for sugar and copra further entrapped the islanders in the growing "Octopus" of "super-capitalism." By the end of the century "depopulation finally makes white settlement safe" (the indigenous population had by then fallen from an estimated 1 million to under 100,000) and "Lever landscape gardens the coast belt with coconut palms." Harrisson reminds us that William Hesketh Lever advertised Sunlight Soap made from copra under the slogan "So Clean"—a cleanliness personified in "a picture by W. P. Frith, the notorious Victorian Academician, famous for his 'Derby Day' and 'Paddington Station,' now so much appreciated as jigsaw puzzles," depicting "an innocent-looking little girl in a white pinafore." Oh, the density of unexpected encounters! As Harrisson was no doubt aware, Lever was a major benefactor of civic institutions in Bolton, the industrialist's hometown.

"We have brought these fine people low," *Savage Civilisation* concludes, "with our twin curses, the germ and the gun ... So, carelessly, we obliterate humans who are unlike ourselves. It is ghastly." Harrisson is less confident of the geography of civility than the *Dictionary of National Biography*. In a preface headed "Jigsaw" he forewarns the reader of the bumpy ride that is to come:

This is not a story of decadence or despair but of inevitability; with oases in chaos. It is a bitter lovely story of man, in stone and song, in iron and gunpowder, seeking in his sequence Tagaro, the sacred Kura bird, a gold beached continent, sweet-scenting sandalwood for Confucius, sugar slaves, the key to Port Sunlight, Pandemonium Government, yellow shoulders nudging for empire, even to the film's last sensationalism—all bloody but (unbelievably) unbowed. And now a smoky phoenix.

I have left each reader to draw most of his own morals and comparisons; of these there are, I believe, many to be drawn. These *Shorter Oxford Dictionary* (1933) definitions should be borne in mind:

Savage: uncivilised; existing in the lowest state of culture.

Civilis (z) ation: the action or process of civilising or being civilised

Civilise: to make civil; to bring out of a state of barbarism, to instruct in the arts of life ...

This is followed not with a Table of Contents but a list of inscrutable headings—Sweet-Smelling, Blackbirds, Depop., Perilously Yellow, Ironic—titled "Pattern in Chaos."

8
The Anthropology of Ourselves

The dissecting table upon which Harrisson would meet Jennings and Madge was the letters page of the *New Statesman and Nation*. On 12 December 1936 a letter appeared there calling for "that anthropological study of our own civilisation of which we stand in such desperate need" in order to shed light on the "primitive" public reaction to Edward VIII's abdication. Madge responded in a letter published on 2 January 1937 indicating that a group had already been formed for this purpose (he meant himself and Jennings, Kathleen Raine, David Gascoyne, and the filmmaker Stuart Legg). He warned that because "English anthropology ... has to deal with elements so repressed that only what is admitted to be a first-class upheaval brings them to the surface ... Fieldwork, i.e. the collection of evidence of mass wish-situations," would have to "proceed in a more roundabout way than the anthropologist has been accustomed to in Africa or

Australia." Nevertheless "clues to these situations might turn up in the popular phenomenon of the coincidence," which he saw as a repressed manifestation of a "hidden wish" amenable to explanation through "the accepted principles" of anthropology and psychoanalysis. "Only mass observations," he concluded, "can create mass science." Coincidence did strike, though not quite in the way Madge envisaged. The only poem Tom Harrisson published in his life ("*For I have a brother, a black hard brother/away in the jungles where no white bibbler ever goes*") appeared directly below Madge's letter in the *New Statesman* under the title "Coconut Moon: A Philosophy of Cannibalism, in the New Hebrides." Serendipity worked its magic. The umbrella and the sewing machine made love. Harrisson contacted Madge and Mass-Observation was born.

Madge, Jennings, and Harrisson announced the foundation of the fledgling organization in another letter to the *New Statesman* on 30 January 1937, which ran under the headline "Anthropology at Home." "We are [...] working out a complete plan of campaign," they informed readers, "which will be possible when we have not fifty but 5,000 observers. The following are a few examples of problems that will arise"—

Behaviour of people at war memorials.
Shouts and gestures of motorists.
The aspidistra cult.
Anthropology of football pools.
Bathroom behaviour.
Beards, armpits, eyebrows.
Anti-semitism.
Distribution, diffusion and significance of the dirty joke.
Funerals and undertakers.

Female taboos about eating.
The private lives of midwives.

It is a gloriously surreal enumeration, reminiscent of Borges' classification of animals in a mythical Chinese encyclopedia that had Michel Foucault spluttering with laughter at the beginning of *The Order of Things*—a laughter, Foucault says, that "shattered ... all the familiar landmarks of my thought—*our* thought, the thought that bears the stamp of our age and our geography—breaking up all the ordered surfaces and all the planes with which we are accustomed to time the wild profusion of existing things."

Within a few weeks over a thousand people had applied to become mass-observers: "coalminers, factory hands, shopkeepers, salesmen, housewives, hospital nurses, bank clerks, business men, doctors and schoolmasters, scientists and technicians." Madge and Jennings organized them into a National Panel, collating their reports from Blackheath. Harrisson meantime recruited a team to carry out a participant-observation study of "Worktown" (as William Hesketh Lever's Bolton now became). The mass-observers' main task was to keep an account of everything they did from waking until sleeping on the twelfth day of every month throughout the year—the so-called day surveys. It so happened that the coronation of George VI fell on 12 May 1937, and the day surveys for that date formed the basis of Mass-Observation's first book, *May the Twelfth*. Though the original intention had been to focus on "normal routine events" Madge and Harrisson believed that this fortuitous coincidence of the day survey with "one event, which affected the whole country" would be "an advantage in the first published example of the method in action."

Mass-Observation was throwing down an epistemological gauntlet. "The original purpose of the Day Surveys," wrote Madge and Harrisson, "was to collect a mass of data without any selective principle." "Mass-Observation," they explained, "has always assumed that its untrained Observers would be *subjective cameras, each with his or her distortion*," who "tell us not what society is like, but what it looks like to them." This clearly resonates with André Breton's claim in the *Manifesto of Surrealism* that

> we, who have made no effort whatsoever to filter ... in our works have made ourselves into *simple receptacles of so many echoes, modest recording instruments* who are not mesmerized by the drawings we are making ... ask me, who was unable to keep myself from writing the serpentine, distracting lines of this preface.

If we listen carefully, we might also hear the distant call of the Great Crested Grebe.

Mass-Observation's aim was not to collect data for the sake of it, as many of their critics charged, but to "counteract the tendency so universal in modern life to perform all our actions through sheer habit, with as little consciousness of our surroundings as though we were walking in our sleep." "Even the drab and sordid features of industrial life," Madge and Harrisson continue, "will take on a new interest when they become the subject of scientific investigation. His squalid boarding-house will become for the observer what the entrails of the dogfish are to the zoologist—the material of science and the source of its *divina voluptas*." This remarkably surrealist image admirably captures the poetics as well as the politics of Mass-Observation. Day surveys were a means of re-enchanting the everyday, as

Madge and Jennings wrote elsewhere, that would be open to all:

> In taking up the role of observer, each person becomes like Courbet at his easel, Cuvier with his cadaver, and Humboldt with his continent. The process of observing raises him from subjectivity to objectivity. *What has become unnoticed through familiarity is raised into consciousness again.*

It is not surprising that such miscegenation of art, science, and politics—not to mention an unsettling confusion of observers and observed—got up academic noses. Noting that they "did not encumber themselves with ... a heavy outfit of methodological scruple, conceptual precision or terminological consistency," Bronislaw Malinowski sniffed at Mass-Observation's "rough and perhaps crude empiricism." He criticizes their "inchoate observation of everything" and inability to make "a clear distinction between the relevant and the adventitious." Raymond Firth, who succeeded Malinowski as Professor of Social Anthropology at the London School of Economics in 1944, ridiculed Mass-Observation's lack of "a clearly stated plan of inquiry" or "precision in the methods employed," accusing them of "presenting a great mass of facts on many points that have not hitherto been empirically studied [that is] not well integrated, nor linked up with the problem they have stated to be the particular subject of their investigation." In *May the Twelfth*, he complains,

> description of Coronation activities is interlarded continuously with remarks on the weather, accounts of people's health, or babies or toilet, or argument about women cyclists or art ... This non-selective

attitude means that the authors have not formulated
their theoretical position at all clearly.

It is remarkable how the cookie-cutter research recipe
has not changed in seventy-five years.

Firth castigates Mass-Observation for burying
"what to an anthropologist are essential phases of the
phenomenon, namely the complex ritual involved, the
religious and moral precepts associated with kingship,
and the political structure which gives the framework
for the ceremony" under "masses of irrelevant crude
fact." What seems not to have occurred to him—but is
abundantly revealed by the dense and disorderly ethno-
graphies thrown up by Mass-Observation's scattergun
methodology—is that quite possibly these are not the
"essential phases of the phenomenon" (or that indeed
there is no singular phenomenon to be studied at all).
The data presented in *May the Twelfth* suggest that a
modern coronation may (also) be many other things,
among them just a good day out. It is harder to distin-
guish between "the sociological law of universal valid-
ity on the one hand, and sundry happenings and
subjective reactions on the other" than Malinowski
assumes. Part of the complexity of social phenomena
lies in their *different* significance to differently located
subjects, a multivalence that gets lost in Firth's search
for that perennial object of sociological desire, a
"representative objective record of real opinion."

It may seem an improbable leap from here to
Émile Durkheim's *Rules of Sociological Method* but this
is after all a discussion of surrealism and the human
sciences. And Durkheim inspired not only positivist
American sociology but also the Collège de sociologie:
Leiris once complained to Bataille that "serious
offenses against the rules of sociological method estab-

lished by Durkheim—whose spirit we continually invoke—have been committed many times at the College." "*The first and most basic rule is to consider social facts as things*," said Durkheim. By this he meant "to treat them as *data*," about whose *essential* nature we cannot presume to know anything a priori. The corollary is that sociologists must "*systematically discard all preconceptions*"—which is exactly what Mass-Observation's rudely unscientific methodology does. As Harrisson, Jennings, and Madge put it in their letter to the *New Statesman*,

> The subject demands the minimum of prejudice, bias and assumption; the maximum of objectivity. It does not presuppose that there are any inexplicable things. Since it aims at collecting data before interpreting them, *it must be allowed to doubt and re-examine the completeness of every existing idea about "humanity,"* while it cannot afford to neglect any of them.

The resulting recordings of the aspidistra cult, the secret lives of midwives, and the anthropology of football pools are the sociological equivalent of Campbell's Siberian negatives—the absolute Particular, the sovereign Contingency, timebombs ticking away in the archives primed to blow apart our presumptions of coherence, identity, and order in the social world.

9
Surrealist Histories

"*May the Twelfth*, with its quotations from Confucius, Shakespeare, Baudelaire and Freud, is actually closer to a surrealist collage than a documentary," remarks Kevin Jackson; "it is about the unofficial, 'unconscious' mind of Britain on its most ceremonial day." Is there a paradigm here for a mode of exposition that does not force the world into Bataille's academic frock-coat but preserves Barthes' "vast disorder of objects," Foucault's "wild profusion of existing things," Campbell's "life as it is lived, not as it is written"? Mass-Observation's "subjective cameras, each with his or her distortion," bring "society" to visibility not as a singular reified abstraction but in a multiplicity of images shot by a multitude of differently situated observers—something that is always in flux and can never be described either in its totality or independently of the biases of one or another point of view. These images are not put forward as illustrations of a thesis or evidence supporting an argument. *They are the argument.* The point is not to make the world artificially coherent in order to render it comprehensible. The ashes and dirt remain.

I am not the first to notice an affinity between *May the Twelfth* and the work of another snapper-up of unconsidered trifles, Walter Benjamin: not only in his famously unfinished *Arcades Project*, but also in such earlier published texts as "One-Way Street." Benjamin's attempt to grasp the world via a spiraling proliferation of fragments was a considered and rigorous methodology, appropriate to the subject matter with which he was dealing. Form followed function. "Method of this project: literary montage," he writes in *The Arcades Project*. "This work," he says, "has to develop to the highest degree the art of citing without quotation marks." *The Arcades Project* is made up of hundreds of passages taken verbatim from the most heterogeneous of sources—found objects, we might very well call them—interspersed with Benjamin's own observations (which are as fragmentary as his sources). Though Benjamin loosely gathers these extracts into folders or "convolutes" he offers no roadmap and few signposts. "I needn't *say* anything. Merely *show*," he believes. "I shall purloin no valuables, appropriate no ingenious formulations. But the rags, the refuse—these I will not inventory but allow, in the only way possible, *to come into their own*, by making use of them." Like Mass-Observation he trusted his subjects to speak for themselves.

"In what way is it possible to conjoin a heightened graphicness ... to the realization of the Marxist method?" Benjamin asks. His answer is that "The first stage in this undertaking will be to carry over the principle of montage into history. That is, to assemble large-scale constructions out of the smallest and most precisely cut components. Indeed, to discover in the analysis of the small individual moment the crystal of the total event." Unfortunately for academics who want to force the universe into a frock-coat, the resulting "large-scale construction" bears less resemblance to Marx's *Capital* than to a Dada collage—Hannah Höch's "Cut with the Kitchen Knife Dada through the Last Weimar Beer-Belly Cultural Epoch of Germany," perhaps, in which "wheels with cogs and gears, automobiles and dancers are juxtaposed with the potentates of the Reich, the men of the empire, and those of the Weimar Republic" while "a pensive Albert Einstein observes the turbulent dynamism of the Berlin metropolis, reduced to a giant weightless mechanism" and "the celebrated Berlin dancer Niddy Impekoven ... seems to breath into the composition its dynamism with a single stag leap." We might note in passing that the kitchen-knife is generally (and was most certainly in 1920s Berlin) a feminine instrument.

As with Mass-Observation, Benjamin's politics and epistemology are intertwined. His aim is not to produce an analysis or explanation of an epoch so much as an *image*—or better, perhaps, a kaleidoscope of images—of that epoch through which "not-yet-conscious knowledge of what has been" is transformed into "something that just now first happened to us, first struck us," a mirror in which we can recognize ourselves anew. Like Madge and Jennings, Benjamin wished to awaken people from their everyday sleepwalking: to "illuminate the darkness of the lived moment" with "the flash of awakened consciousness," breaking "the cycle of the eternally selfsame, until the collective seizes upon [these images] in politics and history emerges." He gave the term *image* a very specific inflection:

It's not that what is past casts its light on what is present, or what is present its light on what is past; rather, *image is that wherein what has been comes together in a flash with the now to form a constellation*. In other words, image is dialectics at a standstill. For while the relation of the present to the past is a purely temporal, continuous one, the relation of what-has-been to the now is dialectical: is not progression but *image*, suddenly emergent.

This "moment of awakening," he argues, "is identical with the 'now of recognizability' *in which things put on their true—surrealist—face.*"

The Impact of Machines, the 1938 exhibition Humphrey Jennings co-organized at the London Gallery, brought engineers' drawings and popular caricatures together with artworks that evidenced the machine's "impact on modern painting" by Duchamp, Léger, Picabia and others. *London Bulletin* devoted a special double issue to the occasion, for which Jennings provided a collage of "texts on the Impact of the Machine" under the title "Do Not Lean Out of the Window." These in turn served as the basis of a series of talks on the Industrial Revolution he gave at a Miner's Institute in Cwmgiedd in Wales by way of a thank you for the community's cooperation in the making of his film *The Silent Village*. Jennings continued to collect material on the impact of the machine for the rest of his life (he died in 1950, falling off a cliff in Greece while scouting a film on postwar healthcare in Europe). This mélange of extracts from letters, diaries, poems and novels, newspapers, scientific journals, and official reports eventually came to rival Benjamin's *Arcades Project*. Jennings's daughter Marie-Louise and Charles Madge published a posthumous (and much abridged) edition of the unfinished work in

1985 under the title *Pandaemonium 1660-1886: The Coming of the Machine as Seen by Contemporary Observers*. *Pandaemonium* would go on to achieve improbable fame as the inspiration for Danny Boyle's spectacular opening ceremony at the 2012 London Olympic Games, which was appropriately titled "Isles of Wonder." Taken from Milton's *Paradise Lost* (which furnishes the first extract in the book), Jennings's title is an apt one in all senses: applying Mass-Observation's method of subjective cameras to the past, he let slip a pandemonium of voices to play havoc with orderly historical narratives.

Introducing the book, Marie-Louise Jennings corrects any misconception that "*Pandaemonium* was an anthology. It is not ... its composition can be compared to a film: each piece moves on to the next, telling a story which never stops. My father used the word 'image' constantly," she explains, "whether about film, painting or writing." David Gascoyne concurs, adding that "Humphrey Jennings's conception of the all-importance of the image" was also "the keystone of Surrealist and most other modern French poetry and painting." So far as I am aware, the historian Michael Saler is the first to have grouped *Pandaemonium* together with Benjamin's *Arcades Project* as examples of a distinct genre he identifies as "surrealist histories." What defines this genre, he writes, is "the juxtaposition of seemingly unrelated texts and images as a way to reveal underlying associations, indirect connections, and unexpected relations," whose objective was to "provide an unmediated narrative, in which the diverse sources spoke for themselves, rather than being spoken for by an omniscient author." Both Benjamin and Jennings, he argues, sought to develop forms of writing "intended to protect *the polyphony of human experience apart from the univocal constraints of analytic reason.*"

"In this book I present the imaginative history of the Industrial Revolution," Jennings explains in his draft introduction to *Pandaemonium*; "Neither the political history, nor the mechanical history, nor the social history nor the economic history, but the imaginative history." "I say 'present', not describe or analyse," he adds in best Benjaminian fashion, "because the Imagination is a function of man whose traces are more delicate to handle than the facts and events and ideas of which history is usually constructed ... *I present it by means of what I call Images*":

> These are quotations from writings of the period in question ... which either in the writing or in the nature of the matter itself or both have revolutionary and symbolic and illuminatory quality. I mean that *they contain in little a whole world*—they are the knots in a great net of tangled time and space—the moments at which the situation of humanity is clear—even if only for the flash time of the photographer or the lighting.

Jennings's images are "moments ... at which clashes and conflicts suddenly show themselves with extra clearness, and which through that clearness can stand as symbols for *the whole inexpressible uncapturable process.*" And this is surely what has been at stake throughout this discussion: developing methodologies capable of giving voice to "the whole inexpressible uncapturable process" *through* the relentless indication of specificity.

The similarities between both the montage form of *The Arcades Project* and *Pandaemonium* and the ways in which Benjamin and Jennings respectively theorize their practice, especially with regard to what they both call *the image*, are striking. Everything indicates that they arrived at their conclusions independently of one another. Jennings could not possibly have read *The Arcades Project*, whose unfinished text Benjamin left with his good friend George Bataille when he fled Paris the day before the city fell to Hitler's armies in 1940. Bataille hid the manuscript in the archives of the Bibliothèque nationale de France for the duration of the war and it remained unpublished until 1982. It was translated into English in 1999, just in time to shed its splintered illumination on a new millennium. Is Jennings's remarkable echo of Benjamin another petrifying surrealist coincidence? Could it just be that *The Arcades Project* and *Pandaemonium* are both expressions of something in the zeitgeist—a shared intimation, perhaps, that the "true face of things" is surrealist? "The owl of Minerva," as Hegel famously observed, "takes its flight only when the shades of night are gathering."

It certainly looks that way from the vantage point of a more recent candidate for admission to Michael Saler's pantheon of surrealist histories. Published in Spanish in 1982-6 and translated into English in 1985-8, Eduardo Galeano's trilogy *Memory of Fire* tells the story of another of those regions of the world whose comprehensive disordering was the other side of making western history coherent. Contemplating Paul Klee's "Angelus Novus," Benjamin imagined the angel of history caught in "a storm ... blowing from Paradise," which "drives him irresistibly into the future, to which his back is turned, while the pile of debris before him grows toward the sky." He ends: "What we call progress is *this* storm." Like Tom Harrisson in *Savage Civilisation* (with which *Memory of Fire* shares a disregard for literary niceties in favor of keeping "the pattern of words to fit the pattern in fact; *angular fact*"), Galeano rummages through the debris the angel's progress leaves in its wake, unearthing encounters of profound density: Mayan myths and Catholic rituals, gold and guano, slavery and smallpox, chocolate and whips.

Reviewing *Memory of Fire* for *The New York Times*, Ronald Christ began:

> Long after Octavio Paz observed that the fragment is the form of our times, we know, with special reference to Latin America, that *it is the content too.* From its fractured map to its splintering factions and classes to its ruptured history, Latin America suggests identity drawn and quartered.

Seizing "this equivalence of form and content," he argues, Galeano's works "invent genre," "smashing categories and joining fragments to yield a 'voice of voices.'" The latter phrase is Galeano's own. "I don't know to what literary form this voice of voices belongs," he says in the (very) brief Preface to *Genesis*, the opening volume of the trilogy. Not that it bothers him. "*Memory of Fire* is not an anthology, clearly not; but I don't know if it is a novel or essay or epic poem or testament or chronicle or ... Deciding robs me of no sleep. I do not believe in the frontiers that, according to literature's customs officers, separate the forms." Galeano pretends neither to objectivity nor impartiality: "Unable to distance myself, I take sides." But on one point he is adamant: "each fragment of this huge mosaic is based on a solid documentary foundation. *What is told here has happened*, although I tell it in my style and manner." It is difficult to shut out the echo of Goya's anguished "*Yo lo vi*" (I saw it) in his *Disasters of War*.

By his own admission "a wretched history student," Galeano set out to "rescue the kidnapped memory of all America, but above all of Latin America" from a "History [that] had stopped breathing: betrayed in academic texts, lied about in classrooms, drowned in dates, they had imprisoned her in museums and buried her, with floral wreaths, beneath statuary bronze and monumental marble." The Uruguayan writer wrote the trilogy during his second exile—a military coup in Montevideo drove him to Buenos Aires in 1973, whence a military coup in 1976 drove him across the Atlantic Ocean in the opposite direction to the course André Breton and Claude Lévi-Strauss took in 1941. He wound up in Madrid where General Francisco Franco, who had ruled Spain since the Civil War, had fortuitously passed away the year before.

Memory of Fire makes its rough music out of more than 1200 images, each as indelible as the disemboweled cow hanging in the rising sun that stayed with André Breton long after the *Capitaine Paul-Lemerle* had docked in Fort-de-France:

1537: Rome

The Pope Says They Are Like Us

Pope Paul III stamps his name with the leaden seal, which carries the likenesses of St. Peter and St. Paul, and ties it to the parchment. A new bull issues from the Vatican. It is called *Sublimis Deus* and reveals that Indians are human beings, endowed with soul and reason.

1625: Samayac

Indian Dances Banned in Guatemala

The monks proclaim that no memory or trace remains of the rites and ancient customs of the Verapaz region, but the town criers grow hoarse proclaiming the succession of edicts of prohibition.

Juan Maldonado, judge of the Royal Audiencia, now issues in the town of Samayac new ordinances *against dances injurious to the Indians' consciences and to the keeping of the Christian law they profess*, because such dances *bring to mind ancient sacrifices and rites and are an offense to Our Lord*. The Indians squander money on feathers, dresses, and masks and *lose much time in rehearsals and drinking bouts, which keep them from reporting for work at the hacienda, paying their tribute, and maintaining their households*.

Anyone dancing the tun will get a hundred lashes ...

1908: San Andrés de Sotavento

The Government Decides
That Indians Don't Exist

The governor, General Miguel Marino Torralvo, issues the order for the oil companies operating on the Colombian coast. *The Indians do not exist*, the governor certifies before a notary and witnesses. Three years ago, Law No. 1905/55, approved in Bogotá by the National Congress, established that Indians did not exist in San Andrés de Sotavento and other Indian communities where oil had suddenly spurted from the ground. Now the governor merely confirms the law. If the Indians existed, they would be illegal. Thus they are consigned to the cemetery or exile.

10
Anne Boleyn's Clock

Let me save the last dance for Horace Walpole—whose eighteenth-century England was, of course, bound body and soul to Galeano's Americas by sugar and slavery, whips and chocolate. "Where the Gothic Castle now stands," begins Walpole's *Description of the Villa ... with an Inventory of the Furniture, Pictures, Curiosities &c.*, "was originally a small tenement, built in 1698, and let as a lodging house." Walpole leased the Twickenham property in 1747 from "Mrs Chenevix, the noted toy-woman." Two years later he bought Strawberry Hill (as he renamed the house) and began to transform it into what he described—with self-conscious irony—as "the castle I am building of my ancestors." The work went on in fits and starts until 1776. Michael Snowdin writes that Walpole's "little plaything-house" that he "got out of Mrs Chenevix's shop" was "the first building to be Gothic inside and outside, and to be a real house ... So it launched the

Gothic Revival and led to buildings such as the Houses of Parliament." Strawberry Hill has also been claimed as the improbable inspiration for Victoria Station in Mumbai, the Town Hall in Vienna, and the Parliament building in Budapest. It is tempting to see a metaphor here for the way in which modern societies routinely confabulate their pasts into national histories, only without Walpole's wit and self-awareness.

"I am almost as fond of the Sharawaggi, or Chinese want of symmetry, in buildings as in grounds or gardens," Walpole informed Horace Mann on 25 February 1750. According to Christopher Tunnard (who approvingly quotes Walpole), "The theorists of Sharawadgi had no faith in mathematics and deified irregularity; [they] found beauty in infinite variety and treated natural material according to that material's own potential organic pattern." A more benign version of Georges Bataille's *informe*, perhaps? The floor plan of Strawberry Hill is asymmetrical to the point of anarchy, "giving the impression of the accretions of age that generations had added." With plentiful imitation of ancient stonework in wood, plaster, and papier-mâché, there is something decidedly postmodern about Walpole's confection.

The "roof, battlement and mantelpieces [were] bristling with spires and gargoyles ... [The] passage-ways and library ceilings were embellished with imagined ancestors, and windows glitter with stained glass collected by the crate load from across Europe." Hallways "were deliberately kept dark to create an atmosphere of medieval 'gloomth' (Walpole's word)," only to open theatrically on "the dazzling brightness of the gallery ... with its ceiling of gold and white plaster and papier mâché, and walls of red damask." Bookcases, chimneybreasts, and other fixtures incorporated details from Old St Paul's, Salisbury and Rouen cathedrals, St Albans abbey, and the chapter house at York. The chimneypiece in the Round Drawing Room, writes Walpole, was "taken from the tomb of Edward the Confessor [in Westminster Abbey], improved by Mr. [Robert] Adam, and beautifully executed in white marble inlaid with scagliuola, by Richter." To the chagrin of Victorian Gothic revivalists like Augustus Pugin, while all this undoubtedly contributed to the "air of enchantment and fairyism, which is the tone of the place," Walpole was indifferent to questions of historical authenticity—whatever *that* might mean—in regard to scale, materials or function.

A gigantic cabinet of curiosities, Strawberry Hill deserves a place of honor among James Clifford's curious collections. Its highlights included rare books, prints, coins, and ceramics (670 items in the small China Closet alone), paintings and drawings (Rembrandt, Van Dyck, Poussin, Reynolds, Canaletto, Giorgione, Holbein, Rubens, Watteau, Lely, van der Weyden), and a collection of miniatures Walpole considered "the largest and finest in any country." Side by side with these—and exhibited in the same equalizing plane, like an advert for a Châtelet show alongside an Old Master in Bataille's *Documents*—Walpole boasted a pair of gloves belonging to James I, the spurs worn by King William in the Battle of the Boyne, and a lock of hair of Edward IV, "cut from his corpse in St George's Chapel at Windsor" (which would later be joined by "a locket with hair of Mary Tudor, Queen of France; whose tomb was opened in 1784; a present from miss Fauquier"). In a niche on the staircase stood "The armour of Francis 1st. king of France, of steel gilt, and covered with bas-reliefs in a fine taste; his lance is of ebony inlaid with silver; his sword steel;

beautifully inlaid with gold, probably the work of Benvenuto Cellini: there is also the armour for the horse's head." Other rooms contained "a tile from the kitchen of William the Conqueror at Caen in Normandy," "Henry VIII's dagger, of Turkish work," "the red hat of Cardinal Wolsey, found in the great wardrobe by Bishop Burnet when clerk of the closet," and—a distant echo of Galeano's *Memory of Fire*—an Aztec mirror "of kennel-coal, in a leathern case ... curious for having been used to deceive the mob by Dr. Dee, the conjurer, in the reign of queen Elizabeth."

Though Strawberry Hill disorders *our* hierarchies of significance, *our* thought, the thought that bears the stamp of our age and our geography, we should not infer that Walpole was by any means an indiscriminate collector—and still less a dilettante. He was unusually concerned to establish the provenance of his acquisitions, and he seems to have known each object intimately. Many told stories. In the China-Room stood

> Two Saxon tankards, one with Chinese figures, the other with European. These tankards are extremely remarkable. Sir Robert Walpole drank ale; the duchess of Kendal, mistress of king George the first, gave him the former. A dozen or more years afterwards, the countess of Yarmouth, mistress of king George the second, without having seen the other, gave him the second; and they match exactly in form and size.

On a more sinister note, in the Green Closet, amid needlework reproductions of Dutch landscapes, views of Roman ruins, and plentiful likenesses of aristocrats, hung "A portrait of Sarah Malcolm, who was hanged for murdering her mistress and two other women in the Temple. She is sitting at a table in Newgate with popish heads before her. This was drawn by Hogarth the day before her execution, and she had put on red to look the better." Can there be a better example of a Barthesian *punctum* than that red?

Apart from Goya, Hogarth is the only visual artist of the past André Breton credits in his *Anthology of Black Humor* with (occasionally) expressing humor "in its pure and manifest state," undiluted by the "degrading influence" of "satiric and moralizing intentions." Pushed by the young Breton to define what he called *umor*, Jacques Vaché responded: "I believe it is a sensation—I almost said a SENSE—that too—of the theatrical (and joyless) pointlessness of everything." Black humor, "the mortal enemy of sentimentality, which seems to lie perpetually in wait," would seem to be the only possible response to another of Walpole's curiosities, which was displayed in the Strawberry Hill library. That this object was an accidental *vanitas* makes it all the more suited to meditation concerning the precarious fate of so many little human constructions:

> A clock of silver gilt, richly chased, engraved and ornamented with fleurs de lys, little heads, &c. on the top sits a lion holding the arms of England, which are also on the sides. This was a present from Henry VIII. to Anne Boleyn; and since, from lady Elizabeth Germaine to Mr. Walpole. On the weights are the initial letters of Henry and Anne, within true lovers knots; at top, *Dieu et mon Droit*.

For those unacquainted with the intertwining of the personal and the political in British royal beds, Henry VIII married Anne Boleyn in 1533 in defiance of Pope Clement VII's refusal to grant him a divorce from his first wife, Catherine of Aragon. The Vatican promptly excommunicated Henry, who countered by declaring himself Supreme Head of the Church of England (under God) by act of parliament. Historians have disagreed ever since over the significance of the ensuing Tudor revolution in government, but it is at least arguable that both the English Reformation and the enormous enhancement it brought to the machinery of the emergent modern state—momentous historical events by any conventional criteria—were accidental by-products of Henry's *amour fou*. Not that those true lovers' knots deterred him from having Anne arrested, tried, and beheaded three years later on charges that included treason, adultery, incest, and witchcraft. After all *Dieu et mon Droit*, the motto of British monarchs then and now, means "God and my right."

Why does Anne Boleyn's clock bring to mind—in the meandering, disorderly, umbrella-and-sewing-machine way of cabinets of curiosities—Klement Gottwald's fur cap: another unforgettably surreal image, with which Milan Kundera opens *The Book of Laughter and Forgetting*?

In February 1948, Communist leader Klement Gottwald stepped out on the balcony of a Baroque palace in Prague to address the hundreds of thousands of his fellow citizens packed into Old Town Square. It was a crucial moment in Czech history—a fateful moment of the kind that occurs once or twice in a millennium.

Gottwald was flanked by his comrades, with Clementis standing next to him. There were snow flurries, it was cold, and Gottwald was bareheaded. The solicitous Clementis took off his own fur cap and set it on Gottwald's head.

The Party propaganda section put out hundreds of thousands of copies of a photograph of that balcony with Gottwald, a fur cap on his head and comrades at his side, speaking to the nation. On that balcony the history of communist Czechoslovakia was born. Every child knew the photograph from posters, schoolbooks, and museums.

Four years later Clementis was charged with treason and hanged. The propaganda section immediately airbrushed him out of history and, obviously, out of all the photographs as well. Ever since, Gottwald has stood on that balcony alone. Where Clementis once stood, there is only bare palace wall. All that remains of Clementis is the cap on Gottwald's head.

Walpole believed "My buildings are paper... and will be blown away in ten years after I am dead." As it turned out, he was wrong. Walpole died in 1797, leaving Strawberry Hill to his cousin's daughter, the sculptress Anne Damer, whence it passed into the Waldegrave family. Lady Frances Waldegrave, the daughter of the renowned Jewish operatic tenor John Braham, inherited Strawberry Hill on the death of her husband George Edward, seventh earl of Waldegrave, in 1846. She enlarged and remodeled the house during the 1850s, adding a "grand Drawing Room, Dining Room, Billiard Room and further accommodation for guests and servants" and "'tudor' chimney pots in the style of Hampton Court" as Strawberry Hill once again became a playground for England's political elite.

Walpole's "Gothic castle" outlived the earnestness of the Victorians and the austerity of twentieth-century modernists, as well as Hitler's Blitz. The estate was eventually purchased by St. Mary's University College in 1923 as a training college for Catholic teachers and Vincentian fathers lived in the house until the 1990s. The Catholic Education service in turn leased the house to the Strawberry Hill Trust. The Trust has recently carried out a wholesale restoration with the help of the Heritage Lottery Fund, aiming "to take the House back to the 1790s at the time of Walpole's death." One room gives a hint of the palimpsest the search for historical authenticity has erased:

> On entering visitors will be able to see Walpole's "Beauty Room" preserved with its various layers exposed: the wooden panelling of the original small house begun in 1698; a gothic fire-place designed for Walpole by Richard Bentley; Walpole's restored windows, shutters and painted glass; a closet with a colourful "bird" paper from the 19th century; a section of William Morris wallpaper dating from the 1930s and an anaglypta ceiling paper from the 1970s! A glass panel in the floor reveals the intricate working of Lady Waldegrave's bell system.

Fate was less kind to the villa's contents. When the Twickenham assizes had the temerity to sentence George Edward Waldegrave (who came into the property in 1835) to six months imprisonment in 1840 for a drunken assault on a policeman, the profligate earl resolved to "sell Walpole's precious collection and let Strawberry Hill rot, as a reproach to the ingratitude of Twickenham." Nineteen-year-old Lady Frances obligingly shared his accommodations in Queen's Bench prison, together with their servants. The Great Sale of 1842 lasted thirty days, scattering Walpole's cabinet of curiosities to the four winds.

Coda:
A Disorganized Mind

In *The Travels and Adventures of Serendipity* Robert Merton and Elinor Barber observe that "there is a kinship between certain historical epochs and a kind of alienation between others; some speak the same basic language, others do not." The nineteenth century found Horace Walpole little to its taste. It was a serious, scientific, and manly age, wont to equate an untidy mind with want of moral character. There is no need here to get sidetracked by the debate as to whether or not Walpole was gay—though he likely was, if, that is, we can apply the category to a time and place in which gay was not an available social identity. For present purposes it suffices to record that he was a life-long bachelor whose "closest friends were women. In them" (in the words of his first biographer Austin Dobson, writing in 1890) "he found just that atmosphere of sunshine and *insouciance*—those conversational 'lilacs and nightingales'—in which his soul delighted, and which were most congenial to his restless intelligence and easily fatigued temperament." A girl's temperament, some would have sneered.

"His mind as well as his house was piled up with Dresden china and illuminated through painted glass," fumed William Hazlitt, "and we look upon his heart to have been little better than a case full of enamels, painted eggs, ambers, lapis-lazuli, cameos, vases, and rock-crystals":

> This may in some degree account for his odd and quaint manner of thinking, and his utter poverty of feeling: He could not get a plain thought out of that cabinet of curiosities, his mind ... He was at all times a slave of elegant trifles, and could no more screw himself up into a decided and solid personage, than he could divest himself of petty jealousies and miniature animosities. In one word, everything about him was little, and the smaller the object and the less its importance, the higher did his estimation and praise of it ascend. He piled trifles to a colossal height— and made a pyramid of nothing "most marvellous to see."

In a disturbingly vicious character assassination (what was he so afraid of?) masquerading as a review of Walpole's letters to Thomas Mann, Thomas Babington Macaulay concurred that for Walpole "Serious business was a trifle, and trifles were his serious business ... The third province, *the Odd*, was his peculiar domain." "He coins new words, distorts the sense of old words, and twists sentences into forms which make grammarians stare," he complains, an evident sign of "an unhealthy and disorganized mind." Macaulay was seriously rattled. God knows what he would have made of Breton and the surrealists. And yet, he concedes,

"Walpole perpetually startles us with the ease with which *he yokes together ideas between which there would seem at first sight to be no connection.*" In this, as in much else, the effeminate trifler who first gave a name to *serendipity* seems to have been well ahead of his time. Walpole possessed a sensibility uncannily attuned to Clifford's world that is permanently surrealist—*our* world—even if that world was then in its infancy and the cultural crisis of modernity more than a century away.

But maybe—as Robert Merton suggested in *Standing on the Shoulders of Giants*—history, too, follows a divagating Shandean course, indifferent to the dictates of ethics, aesthetics, or reason. Whatever we might like to believe, we are such stuff as dreams are made on and it is wise to design our methodologies accordingly. Has anybody ever said it better than Clifford Geertz, writing, as we always do, *After the Fact?*

> One works *ad hoc* and *ad interim*, piecing together thousand-year histories with three-week massacres, international conflicts with municipal ecologies. The economics of rice or olives, the politics of ethnicity or religion, the workings of language or war, must, to some extent, be soldered into the final construction. So must geography, trade, art, and technology. The result, inevitably, is unsatisfactory, lumbering, shaky, and badly formed; a grand contraption. The anthropologist, or at least one who wishes to complicate his transactions, not close them in upon themselves, is a manic tinkerer adrift with his wits: Richard Wilbur's Tom Swift, putting dirigibles together, in the quiet weather, out in the backyard. ■

Bibliography

This is a list of works cited in the text of *Making Trouble*. Full source notes, giving page references for all quotations, can be found on the Prickly Paradigm Press website at: http://www.prickly-paradigm.com

Ades, Dawn and Simon Baker (eds). *Undercover Surrealism: Georges Bataille and DOCUMENTS*. London: Hayward Gallery/Cambridge, MA: MIT Press, 2006.

Agar, Eileen. *A Look at My Life*. London: Methuen, 1988.

André Breton: *42 rue Fontaine*. Paris: Calmelscohen, 2003. Auction catalogue, 8 vols.

Aragon, Louis. *Paris Peasant*. Trans. Simon Watson Taylor. London: Cape, 1987.

Aragon, Louis, Benjamin Péret, and Man Ray. *1929*. Paris: Éditions Allia, 2004.

Bachelard, Gaston. "Surrationalism." In Julien Levy (ed.), *Surrealism*, pp. 186-9.

Bailey, Amanda. "Welcome to the Molly-House: An Interview with Randolph Trumbach." *Cabinet*, No. 8, Fall 2002.

Barr, Alfred (ed). *Cubism and Abstract Art*. New York: Museum of Modern Art, 1986.

—. *Fantastic Art, Dada, Surrealism*. New York: Museum of Modern Art, 1968.

Barron, Stephanie (ed). *"Degenerate Art": The Fate of the Avant-Garde in Nazi Germany*. Los Angeles: Los Angeles County Museum of Art/New York: Abrams, 1991.

Barthes, Roland. *Camera Lucida*. Trans. Richard Howard. London: Vintage, 2000.

Bataille, Georges. *The Absence of Myth: Writings on Surrealism*. Ed. and trans. Michael Richardson. London: Verso, 2006.

—. *Visions of Excess*. Ed. Allan Stoekl. Minneapolis: University of Minnesota Press, 2004.

Bataille, Georges and Michel Leiris. *Correspondence*. Ed. Louis Yvert, trans. Liz Heron. Oxford: Seagull Books, 2008.

Bataille, Georges et al. *Encyclopedia Acephalica*. Ed. Alastair Brotchie. London: Atlas Press, 1995.

Baudelaire, Charles. *The Painter of Modern Life and Other Essays*. Trans. Jonathan Mayne. New York: Phaidon, 2005.

Bee, Harriet S. and Michelle Elligott (eds). *Art in Our Time: A Chronicle of the Museum of Modern Art.* New York, Museum of Modern Art, 2004.

Benjamin, Walter. *The Arcades Project.* Ed. Roy Tiedemann, trans. Howard Eiland and Kevin McLaughlin. Cambridge, MA: Harvard University Press, 1999.

—. *Selected Writings: Volume 1.* Ed. Marcus Bullock and Michael W. Jennings. Cambridge, MA: Harvard University Press, 1996.

—. *Selected Writings: Volume 4.* Ed. Howard Eiland and Michael W. Jennings. Cambridge, MA: Belknap Press of Harvard University Press, 2003.

Bonnet, Marguerite (ed). *Vers l'action politique: Juillet 1925-avril 1926.* Archives de surréalisme, 2. Paris: Gallimard, 1988.

Brassaï. *Conversations with Picasso.* Trans. Jane-Marie Todd. Chicago: University of Chicago Press, 2002.

Breton, André. *Anthology of Black Humor.* Trans. Mark Polizzotti. San Francisco: City Lights Books, 1997.

—. *Arcanum 17.* Trans. Zack Rogow. Los Angeles: Sun and Moon Press, 1994.

—. *Free Rein.* Trans. Michel Parmentier and Jacqueline d'Ambroise. Lincoln, NE: University of Nebraska Press, 1995.

—. *The Lost Steps.* Ed. and trans. Mark Polizzotti. Lincoln, NE: University of Nebraska Press, 1996.

—. *Mad Love.* Trans. Mary Ann Caws. Lincoln, NE: University of Nebraska Press, 1987.

—. *Manifestoes of Surrealism.* Trans. Richard Seaver and Helen R. Lane. Ann Arbor: Michigan University Press, 1972.

—. *Martinique: Snake Charmer.* Trans. David W. Seaman. Austin, TX: University of Texas Press, 2008.

—. *Nadja.* Trans. Richard Howard. New York: Grove Press, 1960.

—. *Œvres complètes, vol. 1.* Ed. Marguerite Bonnet. Paris: Gallimard, 1988.

—. *What Is Surrealism? Selected Writings.* Ed. Franklin Rosemont. New York: Pathfinder, 1978.

Breton, André and Paul Éluard. *Dictionnaire abrégé du surréalisme.* Paris: José Corti, 2005.

Caillois, Roger. *The Edge of Surrealism: A Roger Caillois Reader.* Ed. Claudine Frank. Durham, NC: Duke University Press, 2003.

—. *Man and the Sacred.* Trans. Meyer Barash. Urbana and Chicago: University of Illinois Press, 2001.

Calder, Angus and Dorothy Sheridan (eds). *Speak for Yourself: A Mass-Observation Anthology 1937-1949*. Oxford: Oxford University Press, 1985.

Campbell, Craig. *Agitating Images: Photography against History in Indigenous Siberia*. Minneapolis: University of Minnesota Press, 2014.

—. "The Ephemerality of Surfaces: Damage and Manipulation in the Photographic Image." In Kyler Zeleny (ed.), *Materialities*, London: Velvet Cell, 2016.

Cartier-Bresson, Henri. *The Decisive Moment*. Berlin: Steidl, 2014.

Caws, Mary Ann, Rudolf Kuenzli, and Gwen Raaberg (eds). *Women and Surrealism*. Cambridge, MA: MIT Press, 1991.

Chakrabarty, Dipesh. *Provincializing Europe: Postcolonial Thought and Historical Difference*. Princeton, NJ: Princeton University Press, 2007.

Christ, Ronald. "Dramas that Scorch," *The New York Times*, October 27, 1985.

Clifford, James. *The Predicament of Culture: Twentieth-Century Ethnography, Literature, and Art*. Cambridge, MA: Harvard University Press, 1988.

Corrigan, Philip and Derek Sayer. *The Great Arch: English State Formation as Cultural Revolution*. Oxford: Blackwell, 1985.

Dalí, Salvador. *The Secret Life of Salvador Dalí*. Trans. Haakon M. Chevalier. New York: Dover, 1993.

Dawidoff, Nicholas. "The Man Who Saw America: Looking back with Robert Frank, the most influential photographer alive." *The New York Times Magazine*, July 2, 2015.

Debord, Guy. "Theory of the *Dérive*." Trans. Ken Knabb. Situationist International Online.

de la Beaumelle, Angliviel, Isabel Monod-Fontaine and Claude Schweisguth (eds). *André Breton: La beauté convulsive*. Paris: Centre Pompidou, 1991.

Diez, Marion (ed). *La Subversion des images: Surréalisme Photographie Film*. Paris: Centre Pompidou, 2009.

Dobson, Austin. *Horace Walpole: A Memoir with an Appendix of Books*. London: Osgood McIlvaine and Co., 1893.

Documents. Facsimile reprint. Paris: Jean-Michel Place, 1991.

Durkheim, Emile. *The Rules of Sociological Method*. Ed. Steven Lukes, trans. W. D. Halls. New York: The Free Press, 1982.

—. *Suicide: A Study in Sociology*. Trans. John Spaulding and George Simpson. Glencoe, IL: The Free Press, 1951.

Durozoi, Gérard. *History of the Surrealist Movement*. Trans. Alison Anderson. Chicago: University of Chicago Press, 2002.

Eggleston, William. *The Democratic Forest*. New York: Doubleday, 1989.

Ernst, Max. "An Informal Life of M.E. (as told by himself to a young friend)." In *Max Ernst*, London: Arts Council of Great Britain, 1991.

—. *Beyond Painting*. Chicago: Solar Books, 2009.

Feyerabend, Paul. *Against Method: Outline of an Anarchist Theory of Knowledge*. London: Verso, 1988.

Firth, Raymond. "An Anthropologists' View of Mass-Observation." *Sociological Review*, vol. 31, no. 2, 1939.

Flynn, Pierce J. *The Ethnomethodological Movement: Sociosemiotic Interpretations*. Berlin: de Gruyter, 1991.

Foucault, Michel. *The Order of Things: An Archaeology of the Human Sciences*. New York: Vintage, 1994.

Frank, Robert. *The Americans*. Berlin: Steidl, 2008.

Galeano, Eduardo. *Memory of Fire*. Trans. Cedric Belfrage. 3 volumes: *Genesis, Faces and Masks*, and *Century of the Wind*. New York: Pantheon, 1985-8.

Garfinkel, Harold. *Studies in Ethnomethodology*. Englewood Cliffs, NJ: Prentice-Hall, 1967.

Garrigues, Emmanuel (ed). *Les jeux surréalistes Mars 1921-Septembre 1962*. Archives du surréalisme, 5. Paris: Gallimard, 1995.

Gascoyne, David. *Selected Prose 1934-1996*. Ed. Roger Scott. London: Enitharmon Press, 1998.

—. *A Short Survey of Surrealism*. London: Enitharmon Press, 2000.

Geertz, Clifford. *After the Fact: Two Countries, Four Decades, One Anthropologist*. Cambridge, MA: Harvard University Press, 1996.

Goya: Caprichos, Desastres, Tauromaquia, Disparates. Reproducción completa de las cuatro series. Barcelona: Gustavo Gilli, 1980.

Gracq, Julien. *42 rue Fontaine: L'atelier d'André Breton*. Paris: Adam Biro, 2003.

Greenberg, Clement. *The Collected Essays and Criticism*. Volume 1. Ed. John O'Brian. Chicago: University of Chicago Press, 1988.

Harrisson, T. H. [Tom] "Coconut Moon: A Philosophy of Cannibalism, in the New Hebrides." *New Statesman and Nation*, 2 January 1937, pp. 12-13.

—. *Savage Civilisation*. London: Victor Gollancz, 1937.

Harrisson, T.H. and P.A.D. Hollom, The Great Crested Grebe Inquiry, 1931, at https://britishbirds.co.uk/wp-content/uploads/article_files/V26/V26_N03/V26_N03_P062_092_A013.pdf

Hegel, G.F.W. *Philosophy of Right*. Trans. S.W. Dyde. Kitchener, Ontario: Batoche Books, 2001.

Highmore, Ben. *Everyday Life and Cultural Theory: An Introduction*. London: Routledge, 2002.

Hollier, Dennis (ed). *The College of Sociology 1937-9*. Minneapolis: University of Minnesota Press, 1988.

Iddon, John. *Strawberry Hill and Horace Walpole: Essential Guide*. London: Scala, 2011.

Jackson, Kevin (ed). *The Humphrey Jennings Film Reader*. Manchester: Carcanet Press, 2004.

Jennings, Humphrey. *Pandaemonium 1660-1886: The Coming of the Machine as Seen by Contemporary Observers*. Ed. Marie-Louise Jennings and Charles Madge. London: Icon Books, 2012.

—. "Who Does That Remind You Of?" *London Bulletin*, No. 6, October 1938.

Jennings, Humphrey and Charles Madge with T. O. Beachcroft, Julian Blackburn, William Empson, Stuart Legg, and Kathleen Raine (eds). *May the Twelfth: Mass-Observation Day-Surveys 1937 by over two hundred observers*. London: Faber and Faber, 1937.

Kachur, Lewis. *Displaying the Marvelous: Marcel Duchamp, Salvador Dalí, and Surrealist Exhibition Installations*. Cambridge, MA: MIT Press, 2001.

Krauss, Rosalind and Jane Livingstone. *L'Amour fou: Photography and Surrealism*. Washington: Corcoran Gallery/New York: Abbeville Press, 1985.

Kuenzli, Rudolph (ed). *Dada*. New York: Phaidon, 2006.

Kundera, Milan. *The Book of Laughter and Forgetting*. Trans. Michael Henry Heim. London: Penguin, 1986.

—. *Testaments Betrayed*. Trans. Linda Asher. New York: HarperCollins, 1995.

La Révolution Surréaliste 1924-1929. Ed. Georges Sebbag. Paris: Jean-Michel Place, 1975.

Le Bon, Laurent (ed). *Dada*. Paris: Centre Pompidou, 2005.

Leiris, Michel. *L'Afrique fantôme*. Paris: Gallimard, 2008.

Lévi-Strauss, Claude. *Anthropology Confronts the Problems of the Modern World*. Trans. Jane Marie Todd. Cambridge, MA: Harvard University Press, 2013.

—. *Tristes Tropiques*. Trans. John Russell. New York: Criterion Books, 1961.

Levy, Julien (ed). *Surrealism*. New York: Da Capo, 1995.

Lewis, C. Day (ed). *The Mind in Chains: Socialism and the Cultural Revolution*. London: Frederick Muller, 1937.

London Bulletin, nos. 4-5, 1938, special double issue on "The Impact of Machines."

Macaulay, Thomas Babington. "Walpole's Letters to Sir Horace Mann." *Edinburgh Review*, vol. 58, 1833.

Madge, Charles. "Bourgeois News." *New Verse*, no. 19, Feb.–March 1936.

—. "The Meaning of Surrealism," *New Verse*, no. 10, 1934.

—. "Surrealism for the English." *New Verse*, no. 6, December 1933.

Madge, Charles and Tom Harrisson. *The First Year's Work*. London: Lindsay Drummond, 1938.

—. *Mass-Observation*. London: Frederick Muller, 1937.

Madge, Charles and Humphrey Jennings. "Poetic Description and Mass-Observation." *New Verse*, no. 24, 1937.

Mahon, Alyce. *Surrealism and the Politics of Eros 1938-1968*. London: Thames and Hudson, 2005.

Merton, Robert K. *On the Shoulders of Giants: A Shandean Postscript*. Chicago: University of Chicago Press, 1993.

Merton, Robert K. and Elinor Barber. *The Travels and Adventures of Serendipity*. Princeton, NJ: Princeton University Press, 2004.

Miller, Lee. *Grim Glory: Pictures of Britain under Fire*. Ed. Ernestine Carter. London: Lund, Humphries, 1941.

Minotaure. Facsimile reprint in 3 vols. Geneva: Skira, 1981.

Moriyama, Daido. *Shinjuku*. Tucson, AZ: Nazraeli, 2002.

Morris, Roderick Conway. "The Gothic Pioneer Horace Walpole Finally Gets His Due." *The New York Times*, March 22, 2011.

New Statesman and Nation, letters page, 12 December 1936, 2 January 1937, 30 January 1937.

New Verse, no. 1, January 1933, editorial headed "Why?"

Owens, Bill. *Suburbia*. New York: FotoFolio, 1999.

Oxford Dictionary of National Biography (online version).

Parr, Martin. *The Last Resort*. London: Dewi Lewis, 2009.

Penrose, Antony (ed.). *Lee Miller's War: Photographer and Correspondent with the Allies in Europe 1944-5*. London: Thames and Hudson, 2005.

Peret, Benjamin. *Remove Your Hat*. Trans. Humphrey Jennings and David Gascoyne. London: Roger Broughton, 1936.

Pierre, José (ed). *Recherches sur la sexualité, janvier 1928-août 1932*. Archives du surréalisme 4. Paris: Gallimard, 1990.

—. *Investigating Sex: Surrealist Discussions 1928-1932*. Trans. Malcolm Imrie. New York: Verso, 1992.

Read, Herbert (ed). *Surrealism*. New York: Harcourt, Brace, and Company, 1937.

Remy, Michel. *Surrealism in Britain*. Aldershot: Ashgate, 1999.

Richardson, Nigel. "Strawberry Hill house: blast from a Gothic past." *Daily Telegraph*, 9 October 2010.

Rosemont, Franklin and Robin D. G. Kelly (eds). *Black, Brown, and Beige: Surrealist Writings from Africa and the Diaspora*. Austin, TX: University of Texas Press, 2009.

Rosemont, Penelope (ed). *Surrealist Women: An International Anthology*. Austin, TX: University of Texas Press, 1998.

Saler, Michael. "Whigs and Surrealists: the 'Subtle Links' of Humphrey Jennings's *Pandaemonium*." In George K. Behlmer and Fred M. Leventhal (eds), *Singular Continuities: Tradition, Nostalgia, and Identity in Modern British Culture*, Stanford, CA: Stanford University Press, 2000.

Sayer, Derek. *The Coasts of Bohemia: A Czech History*. Princeton, NJ: Princeton University Press, 1998.

—. *Prague: Capital of the Twentieth Century: A Surrealist History*. Princeton, NJ: Princeton University Press, 2013.

Sebbag, Georges (ed). *en Jeux surréalistes*. Paris: Jean-Michel Place, 2004.

—. *Enquêtes surréalistes: De Littérature a Minotaure 1919-1933*. 2 vols. Paris: Jean-Michel Place, 2004.

Snodin, Michael (ed). *Horace Walpole's Strawberry Hill*. New Haven, CT: Yale University Press, 2009.

Solomon, Deborah. *Utopia Parkway: The Life and Work of Joseph Cornell*. New York: Farrar, Straus and Giroux, 1997.

Sontag, Susan. "The Art of Fiction." Interview with Edward Hirsch, *The Paris Review*, No. 143, 1994. Available at: http://www.theparisreview.org/interviews/1505/the-art-of-fiction-no-143-susan-sontag (accessed 17 June 2015).

—. *On Photography*. New York: Rosetta Books, 2005.

Soth, Alec. *Songbook*. New York: Mack, 2014.

Soupault, Philippe. *Last Nights of Paris*. Trans. William Carlos Williams. Cambridge, MA: Exact Change, 1992.

Srp, Karel. *Jindřich Štyrský*. Prague: Torst, 2001.

Surrealism: Catalogue. London: Women's Printing Society, 1936.

Thévenin, Paule (ed). *Bureau de recherches surréalistes: Cahier de la permanence Octobre 1924-avril 1925*. Archives du surréalisme 1, Paris: Gallimard, 1988.

Walpole, Horace. *A Description of the Villa of Horace Walpole ... with an Inventory of the Furniture, Pictures, Curiosities &c*. Facsimile edition. London: Pallas Athene, 2015.

—. *Letters of Horace Walpole*. 2 volumes. Ed. Charles Duke Yonge. London: T. Fisher Unwin, 1890.

Weber, Max. *The Protestant Ethic and the Spirit of Capitalism*. Trans. Talcott Parsons. London: Allen and Unwin, 1930.

Zellar, Brad and Alec Soth. *House of Coates*. Minneapolis: Coffee House Press, 2014.

Also available from Prickly Paradigm Press:

continued

continued